MW01031125

Hatch Guide for Lakes

aturals and Their Imitations for Stillwater Trout Fishing

Hatch Guide for Lakes

Naturals and Their Imitations for Stillwater Trout Fishing

Jim Schollmeyer

Frank Amato

PORTLAND

Dedicated to

Frances—my mother—for her love and guidance and Albert—my father—for sharing his tackle and love for fishing lakes with his children and grandchildren.

Acknowledgments

Generous help from the following people made this book possible.

This book was conceived during a brainstorming session with Ted Leeson and his wife Betty Campbell in their Jeep on the drive home after fishing in Montana. Ted's ideas, insights and editing enabled me to produce this book. The Leesons opened their home and hearts to me, and I am glad to call them friends. Rick Hafele, the noted fly fishing entomologist, was always there to answer any questions about insects. Richard Bunse provided his great drawings. Keith Burkhart, owner of The Valley Fly Fisher in Salem, supplied materials and fishing information. The following fly anglers took time to tie their favorite patterns for me: Ted Leeson, Richard Bunse, Lee Clark, Joe Warren, Henry Hoffman, Gary Warren, and Jim Cope.

©1995 Jim Schollmeyer
Book Layout: Alan Reid / Joyce Herbst / Kim Koch
Printed in Hong Kong
Frank Amato Publications, Inc.
P.O. Box 82112 Portland, Oregon 97282
(503)-653-8108
ISBN 1-57188-038-0
Printed in Hong Kong, China
3 5 7 9 10 8 6 4 2

Table of Contents

Chapter 5

Chapter 6

Introduction

Stillwater trout—those in lakes and ponds—actually occupy only a small percentage of the total water available to them. Locating fish can be an intimidating and frustrating experience, particularly if you are accustomed to fishing rivers, where the holding water is more clearly defined. Still, there are clues. Every murder-mystery reader knows that "if you follow the money, you'll find the killer." Likewise, lake anglers understand that "if you follow the food source, you'll find the trout." These food sources take many forms, but they can be loosely divided into two groups—those in control of their movements, and those that drift about controlled by the elements. Most food sources, in fact, shift between these two groups during their life cycles, which makes understanding their habitats, habits, and seasonal rhythms very important for fly anglers in locating and catching trout.

Lake fly fishing is in a constant state of evolution. Only a few generations ago, attractor flies and streamers were the lures of choice for lake fishing, and judging by the old photographs, they caught more than their share of fish. Most of these early flies were trolled behind a rowed or wind-drifted boat. Owing largely to limitations of the tackle, casting was usually confined to shorter distances. But fishing changed with the times. With increasing angling pressure, over-fishing, and at times poor management, the fish grew more cautious, and the old standard flies became less and less effective. Anglers started devising patterns that more closely matched the baitfish and insects they found in their stillwaters. Local experts tied flies that worked at least part of the time, and every lake seemed to have its own special patterns. Of necessity, anglers began paying closer attention to aquatic food forms, particularly insects.

Nowadays, of course, it's hard to find an experienced fly fisherman who isn't familiar with the hatches and habits of the major aquatic insects. And the evolution of tackle has helped him put this knowledge to work. Fly rods, leaders, and especially lines have improved, and today's angler has enormous flexibility in adjusting his fishing methods to match water conditions, depth, and the increasing variety of flies used to imitate stillwater food forms.

For all of our changes, though, the trout still come out ahead much of the time, which is hardly surprising. They've evolved and survived for millennia, learning early the sizes, shapes, colors, habitats, and actions of their prey, and learning in turn that caution and flight are the best defenses against predators. They know their world by instinct. We, however, must observe and study it, with a keen understanding toward the organisms that trout feed upon. Learning the habits of its prey takes time, and this book is intended to help make the process more efficient. But you may find that it opens the door to a flood of new questions, many of which are not answered here. Fortunately, part of the evolution of modern fly fishing is an increasing number of useful books on limnology—the scientific study of the life and phenomena of fresh water lakes and ponds; on aquatic entomology—the scientific study of aquatic insects; and on books devoted to stillwater angling. Such resources have much to teach the fisherman, and learning more about the relationships among trout, their prey, and their environment will not only increase your effectiveness as an angler, but expand the kinds of interest and enjoyment that are held by lakes and ponds.

This book is designed as a basic guide to insect hatches and other food sources in stillwaters. While it isn't comprehensive, it does cover the major groups and will help you fish most lakes intelligently. But as in any kind of fishing, a little advance research pays off. If you're going to a new lake, try to find out as much information about it as possible. Fly shops are unquestionably the best source of information on local lakes. You can usually find out the condition of the water, the most productive times to fish, the most likely areas, the predominant hatches, and the most effective flies to match them. You should also ask if there are any special fishing regulations you should know about, since many lakes now have restrictions in place to protect the resource and habitat. It's pointless, for example, to drag a motor boat across two states only to discover that gasoline engines are prohibited on the water you intend to fish. Or to have a game officer patiently explain, as he hands you a citation, that the two flies on your leader is one too many.

If you're unable to uncover any information before you arrive at a lake, you'll need to conduct a little on-site research. It may mean the difference between a tired wrist from playing fish or a tired arm from fruitless casting. Most fly fishermen are helpful and some of us even like to kibitz a bit, so seek information from anglers that you bump into on shore, at camp, or by a boat ramp. They can be the best guides to success at a given time and place. Anglers on the water, however, don't appreciate being disturbed; respect their privacy and keep your distance from them.

Even if you receive the straight scoop from a fly shop or a helpful fisherman, it pays to do some additional snooping before you start fishing. For this, you'll need a medium size aquarium net, a small white plastic plate, tweezers, and an empty clear-plastic 35mm film canister. Use the net to check the shoreline areas for empty nymphal shucks which have drifted in after emerging insects discarded them in open water. If you find any shucks, put one in the film canister filled with water. The nymphal skin will fill out, taking on the shape of the insect that left it, and you should be able to get a close identification.

Next check the shallows for anything that moves, and try to net it. Again put the specimen in the film canister for a closer look. Try to identify it—note its color and size; observe the way it swims. If it proves to be a minnow, put it back unharmed after studying it; you may have caught a small trout. Drag your net around any weeds that you find and dump the contents on the white plate with a little water. Any captured bugs will stand out as you clear away the plant debris. Use the tweezers to transfer the critter to the film canister for a closer look and identification. Return the weeds and specimen back to the same area they came from once you're finished. Then look carefully for any insects or shucks on weeds or structures protruding above the surface. Some insects crawl out of the water to emerge, leaving their nymphal shucks clinging to plants or objects above the waterline. Collecting one of these dried shells is a good way to identify the insect.

When you've collected a specimen of potential trout food, see if you can locate it in this book. It need not be an exact match. Read the information below the photograph to see if the organism in fact corresponds to the area, season, and habitat in which it was collected. If so, read on to find out more about it. On the facing page, across from the picture of the natural, is a photograph that shows examples of three flies used to imitate what you have collected. You don't have to have an exact imitation, but you should pick one that is close to the size, shape, and color of the natural. The text below the flies will give you information about how, when, and where to fish the fly so it best imitates the living animal.

Should your search turn up nothing, choose a fly pattern that imitates a food item common to the area and time of the year. Then consult the appropriate section of the guide for information on the type of water to look for and the best technique for fishing it.

Chapter 1

Understanding Lakes

Clues for locating trout in stillwaters are less visible than those in rivers or streams. Learning the physical characteristics of a lake is the smartest way to start your fishing trip. Getting a map of the water you plan to fish will make your search for productive areas easier. If there is no map available, make one as you explore; it can be used in the future should you fish the lake again. Construct the map in a scale large enough to add additional information.

With or without a map, though, finding and catching trout in lakes or ponds requires an understanding of stillwater structure and biology.

Lake Geography

Lakes collect water through seepage or drainage. They occur in a variety of terrain types, are found in a wide range of geographical locations, and come in all shapes and sizes. Still, it is possible to generalize about them to some degree.

The geographical location of a lake has a substantial influence on its capacity to support trout year-round. Lakes above 8,000 feet have a short ice-free season in which the trout can grow—if they survive winterkill. Lowland lakes will not support trout if water temperatures exceed the low 80s. The latitude of a lake also has an obvious affect on water temperature. In southern zones, low-altitude lakes become too warm, and in northern zones shallow lakes may freeze over and winterkill. Similarly, insect emergence dates are also affected by latitude and elevation. Lower elevation and southern-zone lakes warm earlier, producing hatches sooner than higher or northern-zone lakes.

A lake has its own local geography as well. The contour of a lake bottom is normally an extension of the character of the land around it. Sharp rises in elevation in the surrounding terrain are a good indication that the lake bed drops off sharply and that the water is deep. Conversely, land that rises gradually from the shoreline usually indicates a shallow lake. Most natural lakes have relatively stable water levels, and those with a large ratio of shoreline and shallows to open water tend to have the largest amount of plant growth. These lakes support greater populations of insects, crustaceans, and trout. The reverse is true of a lake with less shoreline and fewer shallows. The sunlight required for plant growth will not penetrate deep water; if the bottom drops off quickly, there is little opportunity for vegetation to take hold. Man-made lakes—reservoirs and impoundments—are somewhat less predictable than natural ones. Fluctuations in water level due to drawdown restricts plant growth even in the shallows since these areas are sometimes above water and sometimes below it.

Bottoms

Bottoms can be weedy, rocky, sandy, muddy, or any combination of these. Weedy bottoms are often the most productive for fishing and the most dangerous to fragile tippets. Rocky bottoms offer enough cover to hold trout, but any artificial fished along a rocky, fly-grabbing bottom has a short life expectancy. Carry extra flies. Sandy and muddy bottoms offer trout little cover other than depth. They are the easiest to fish, the least demanding on terminal gear, and often the least productive.

Shallows

Shallow areas in a lake are often signaled by the gentle downward slope of the adjacent land. Shallows may run from ankle-high to 10 or 12 feet deep, but they are, day in and day out, the most fertile source of food for trout. Approach this water with caution to avoid spooking fish holding or feeding there. Since trout are less visible and more secure during the low-light periods of morning and evening, these are often the best times to fish the shallows.

Surface-feeding trout are easy to spot in shallow water, and they offer the most challenging and enjoyable fishing on the lake—the kind that every angler fantasizes about but rarely sees. The reality is that trout spend most of their time searching for food that swims or crawls close to the bottom. So that's where you have to fish if you want to catch them. The nymphs of dragonflies, damsels, and some mayflies migrate from deeper water across shallows to the shore or to shoreline vegetation, where they emerge. During these emergence times, trout often patrol shallow water, on the lookout for any insects moving toward shore. Imitate these insects by matching their direction of migration and behavior. Cast your fly from the shore out to deeper water, and use a retrieve—crawling, darting, swimming—that reproduces the motion and speed of the natural. When casting from the shore, use a floating or sink-tip line to keep the body of the fly line off the bottom or out of the shallow-water weeds.

Shoals

Shoals rise up from surrounding deep water, but do not protrude above the water's surface. These sunken islands offer trout the shelter of adjoining deep water and a meal from the creatures that live in its shallow areas. Shoals can often be seen during calm periods as a lighter-colored area surrounding the dark color of deep water. Mark the location of these areas on your map to help find them during times when they are less visible.

Because of the water depth, it is often hard to spot fish around shoals. To avoid spooking trout that hold there, cast to the edges and tops of shoals from a distance. Fish the water in a systematic searching pattern, covering the different levels of water over the shoal. Uniform sinking lines get the fly down quickly and hold the fly at the desired depth as you fish it back.

Springs

Springs may reveal their location as a clear area in a weedy bottom or occasionally by a steady stream of bubbles rising to the surface. Many springs are discovered as the result of the large numbers of fish that gather around them for the comfort of emerging cool water or for the insects that collect on plants that flourish in the spring's mineral rich waters. If the water is shallow enough, you may see a group of trout bunched in one spot, but deep-water springs are often revealed only by the steady supply of trout hooked in a small area.

Finding a spring in a lake is like discovering a good restaurant. You know they exist, but unless you stumble onto one, or some kind soul shows it to you, they are difficult to find. If you are lucky enough to come across a spring, note its location carefully for future visits. Use a sinking line to cover the deep-water springs and floating line for emerging insects or shallow-water springs.

Inlets

Inlet streams are the life blood of most lakes—they add water, nutrients, and food. Beyond the mouths of inlets, shallow bars often form from sediment deposited by the stream. Trout maintain feeding positions in the deep water near these bars to intercept insects and other creatures carried or attracted to the area. If the inlet stream is suitable for spawning, trout congregate near the mouth shortly before running up to spawn. Some of the largest fish in a lake are often hooked during this period. Trout also follow other spawning fish upstream to feed on their spawn or wait at the mouth of the inlet to feed on the young fish as they enter the lake.

Trout generally hold in the still water next to the flowing water, so approach it with care. When you are fishing flies that imitate insects drifting into the lake from an inlet stream, take a position off to one side of the flowing water. Use a floating or sink-tip line and cast quartering up-current, allowing the fly to drift naturally into the lake's quieter water. Cover the closer water first, and extend your drift to cover areas farther away, feeding out and mending line to maintain a drag-free drift.

Baitfish and small trout often gather around inlets, and they can be imitated with a streamer fished on a sink-tip or sinking line. Take a casting position to the side of the inflowing stream; cast the fly up-current, letting it tumble down into quiet water, and then fish it back. Trout often pick up the streamer as it drifts down into deeper water. If your line pauses or makes any unusual movement, lift your rod to tighten up on the line. If there is no resistance, drop the rod and continue the drift.

Outlets

Where a lake narrows to an outlet, insects are collected and funneled out into a stream. Trout take up feeding stations in or near the outlet to intercept any food drifting past. Because the water is often clear and the current moving slowly, fishing for trout around outlets is more like fishing a large spring creek. If you are trying to imitate a dead drifting insect in this water, you will need to cast from a position that allows a long drag-free drift—normally a point off to the side of the outlet flow. A floating line with a long, fine leader gives a better drift of the wet or dry fly.

Baitfish and small trout often congregate near outlets to feed on the abundant food supply. In the deeper waters next to outlets, fishing a streamer on a uniform-sink or sink-tip line can produce some excellent trout that hold there during the day. Evenings, mornings, and windy days provide cover for large trout that venture into the shallows to feed on smaller fish. During these conditions, you should search the shallower water around an outlet with a streamer.

Channels

Lakes formed by streams that have been naturally or artificially dammed have channels of deeper water on the lake bottom marking the course of the old stream bed. Channels running through shallow areas offer excellent holding habitat for trout. The security of deep water in these channels allows trout to move and feed in them at any time. Even extremely cautious trout will leave the shelter of a channel to forage in the adjoining food-rich shallows, knowing the safety of deeper water is close. Channels between lakes or connecting arms of a lake may also afford enough deep water or shelter to become gathering spots for trout traveling through or feeding in them.

Finding flooded river channels is simple in shallow water—just locate a darker band of deep water running through the lighter colored shallows. Locating channels in deeper water requires the use of a depth finder or a sounding line. A line marked at 3 foot intervals with a weight on the end can be lowered to bottom at regular intervals to detect abrupt changes in depth.

To fish a channel, position yourself in the shallows back from the channel's edge. Cast beyond the edge, letting the fly sink into the deeper water, and then fish it back. A floating or sink-tip line works best for this presentation. Trout often take the fly as it starts to climb out of the channel.

Drop-Offs

A "drop-off" is the point at which the depth of a lake increases abruptly. A drop-off located next to a weedy, insect-rich shallow area is a sure bet for trout, since the fish can cruise the edge for food while remaining close to the safety of deeper water. A drop-off is easy to locate; it is signaled by a sudden darkening of the water color owing to the increased depth. In clear water, you often see the bottom drop off.

When light conditions are bright, trout seek the security of deep water at drop-offs, so midday is the best time to fish these waters, especially if they are close to productive feeding areas. To cover the water properly, use a sink-tip or a uniform-sinking line since these will bring a fly to the bottom quickly and keep it there during the retrieve.

Wind

From gentle breezes to gales, winds are part of the make-up of every lake. Without winds most stillwaters would be unable to support trout. Air sweeping across the surface of a lake pushes any insects on or above the water's surface downwind. While strong-flying or lucky insects may escape the wind, the weak and unfortunate end up in the water, where they join an assortment of emerging, emerged, or spent insects already on the surface. This accumulation of trout food in the surface film is thickest along the windward shore or in the windrow-like foam lines that form on the water. Points of land projecting out into the lake form a buffer on the lee side, which creates a seam between the calm, protected water and the rough water of the open lake. This seam is another collecting area for trapped insects. Cliffs or high bluffs on the windward end of a lake offer trout an exceptional feeding area for wind-driven insects that collide with the rock face and drop into the water. A floating or intermediate line will keep the fly in or close to the surface when fishing for trout under windy conditions. When possible position yourself so that your casts quarter upwind and the fly drifts downwind.

Many anglers head for the barn when the wind starts blowing, and they often miss out on fabulous fishing. This, however, does not mean you should stay out in gale force winds if you feel uncomfortable about the weather and water conditions. Never put yourself in danger while floating on stillwater; if your craft is unstable in rough conditions, get off the water when the wind picks up.

Lake Biology

Water Quality

To survive in a lake, a trout has very specific needs. The water temperature must stay below the low 80s in the summer, though temperatures of 70 degrees and lower are more comfortable. Similarly, lakes that freeze over must be deep enough to provide a livable temperature through the winter. Whether in the hot summer season or the snowbound winter months, plants and algae in a lake must produce enough oxygen for trout to survive.

A healthy trout population requires a constant supply of food, which is governed by the fertility of the water. Above-normal water acidity diminishes the productivity of a lake, which in turn reduces the number of plants and fish. Water that is slightly alkaline, on the other hand, promotes productivity and increases biological abundance. A lake's color is a good indicator of fertility. Blue-colored lakes have only small amounts of suspended organic material and less plant growth, resulting in less food for the trout population. Less food simply means fewer or smaller fish—a condition often found in high elevation lakes. Greenish-colored lakes are normally more productive. The suspended organic matter responsible for the green color increases the water's ability to absorb sunlight, promoting plant growth, insect life, and ultimately trout.

Water holds the dissolved oxygen necessary for respiration in animals and the carbon dioxide necessary for photosynthesis in plants, which is the keystone of a lake's richness. Many of the other elements needed to promote the growth of plants and animal life are also held in solution. Water motion helps mix these nutrients, so they can be used by the organisms that inhabit a lake.

Aquatic Vegetation

Plant growth in a lake is vital to the survival of the aquatic animal forms. Wherever water depth and clarity allow the sun's ray to penetrate, phytoplankton will flourish. These small, free-floating aquatic plants feed zooplankton, tiny animal organisms, which are in turn fed upon by insects, crustaceans, and small fish—all of which become prey for larger trout. Moreover, rooted plants provide shelter for many of the lake's inhabitants and play host to a variety of periphyton, organisms such as algae and small crustaceans that live attached to plant surfaces. These organisms then feed many of the insects and larger crustaceans that also live in the weeds. In short, weedy areas produce most of the food in a lake, give shelter to much of it, and draw trout like a magnet.

There are three areas of rooted plant-growth that are important to fish for food and shelter. The first area is at the water's edge where plants such as cattails, reeds, and bulrushes emerge from the water. Though these plants often grow too closely together for larger trout to forage among them, the vast amount of food produced in these areas encourages trout to cruise their edges searching for a careless nymph or baitfish leaving its shelter.

Floating vegetation, the second area, is usually just off shore. These plants include lily pads, arrowheads, and spatterdock. (Duckweed, though not rooted to the lake bottom, is also included in this group.) Floating plants offer overhead cover for all the creatures that inhabit them. When water conditions are right, neither too warm nor too shallow, trout will hunt among these weeds, often nudging or plucking insects and scuds from the stems and bottoms of floating vegetation. Floating vegetation is frequently used by aquatic insects that crawl out of the water to emerge. These plants also provide adult insects a place to rest or a position from which they can crawl back into the water to lay their eggs.

Submerged vegetation is the third type of rooted plant and includes elodea and water milfoils. These plants will grow at any depth that is penetrated by sunlight, from the shoreline well out into open water. Weed beds in shallow water are the easiest to see, though often the most difficult to fish. Use a floating, sink-tip, intermediate, or sinking line to fish your flies over and among these shallow-water weed beds. In these areas, a long leader is necessary to keep the fly line from spooking feeding trout.

Away from the shallows, sunken weed beds can be difficult to spot. Using polarized glasses, try to locate the weedy areas when the water is calm; they will show as darker areas along the bottom. But if poor water clarity, excessive depth, glare, surface chop, or lack of illumination prevent you from seeing submerged vegetation, then you must search them out using your sunken fly to probe the bottom. When the fly snags in the weeds or comes back with vegetation hanging from it, you have found the spot. Insect and scud populations can be very dense in these weed patches, and when the plants are growing in deep water, the trout feel secure while feeding among them. When fishing sunken weed beds, put the fly near or among the weeds to imitate the natural food forms. A uniform-sink or a sink-tip line sinks the fly quickly and keeps it down at the proper depth during the retrieve. During a mayfly or caddis emergence, use a floating line with a long leader and weighted fly to reach to bottom. As you fish it back the fly will rise, imitating a natural leaving the bottom.

Seasonal Cycles

In shallow lakes, those normally less than 20 feet deep, wave action will keep the water well mixed, and its temperature and density remain uniform throughout the lake. The influence of wave action, however, diminishes with depth, and in lakes deeper than 20 feet or so, water temperature and density are not equalized. Waters at different temperatures have different densities, and since these different densities do not mix, the lake forms layers of water in a process called "stratification." As the air temperature changes with seasons, the temperature differential in these layers also changes. As a result, these deeper lakes undergo an annual cycle of "stratification" and "turnover," a process in which the water separates into layers and then re-mixes. Turnover is the result of a lake's water temperature equalizing in all the layers; when this occurs the nutrient rich bottom layer of the lake mixes with the upper layers.

Winter stagnation is the start of the seasonal cycle, and the water temperature in a lake is very nearly the same from top to bottom. The water is cold, causing both insects and trout to slow their activity. Fly anglers normally follow suit.

Spring turnover occurs just after ice-out, when the air temperature begins to rise. The near-freezing surface water begins to warm and becomes, through a small range of temperatures, more dense and heavier than the water below it. The surface layer sinks, combining with the lower layers and distributing a wealth of nutrients from the lake bottom throughout the water, making them available to the plants and animals that can use them. This is a very active time for lakes. Plankton blooms in the open water. Plants in shallows burst into new growth. Insects and crustaceans feed hungrily on the vegetation and on each other. And the trout move in to dine. This is one of the fly angler's most opportune times.

Summer stratification starts after spring turnover. The sun continues to heat the water as the days get longer. The warming surface water becomes less dense than the water below it, finally reaching a point where their densities are too dissimilar to mix. A "thermocline" develops—a strata of water noticeably colder than the layer of water above it. The thermocline and the layer beneath it have low amounts of oxygen and forms a barrier most trout will not cross. As the upper waters warm, trout move closer to the cooler water next to the thermocline when they are not foraging for food. Finding the depth of the thermocline, where trout normally hold during the dog days of summer, may be the only way you will connect with one during daylight hours.

Fall turnover occurs when the upper layer of the lake cools and becomes more dense than the thermocline. The topmost water-layer mixes with the lower layers, and the settled bottom nutrients are again disbursed throughout the lake. New plant growth begins, and insects, crustaceans, and trout go on a final feeding frenzy before winter stagnation starts.

Spring and fall turnovers are the most productive times for a fly angler to fish the shallows of a lake because of the increased activity of the trout's prey. During summer stratification of deeper lakes, surface temperatures are high, and trout are difficult to find unless you locate the level of the thermocline and fish above it. Trout move from this area only to forage for food, which usually happens from evening to just after sunrise.

Chapter 2

Lake Fishing: Tackle and Techniques

Successful lake fishermen are usually those that are the best prepared—by becoming familiar in advance with the water and its hatches, by studying the lay of the lake upon arriving, by acquiring a repertoire of techniques to fish different water types, and by having the tackle suited to those methods.

Lake-Fishing Tackle

Rods

Lake-fishing has some special requirements that depend upon what types of flies you will be fishing and at what depth you fish them. Trout feeding on, or just under, the surface are often taking very small insects, which require correspondingly small imitations and fine tippets. The right rod for surface fishing must allow you to set the hook in a large trout without snapping the lightest tippet you expect to fish, typically 5X or 6X. At the same time, a lake rod must also cast far enough to cover the fish, often 40 to 60 feet away. Many of the powerful rods made today can cast a country mile, but will not handle tippets of 5X or lighter. If you are going to be fishing tippets of this size, look for a rod with a softer tip that will help absorb the shock when setting a hook. Many 4 and 5 weight rods fill the bill.

Rods used for subsurface fishing must be able to cast long distances with a large range of different fly sizes and weights. They should also be able to handle 4X or 5X tippets without breaking on the strike. Rods rated at 5, 6, or 7 weight may all work, with the 6 weight a good all-around choice for most subsurface lake fishing. Go to different weight rods when conditions call for the use of lighter or heavier tippets.

Rods used for lake fishing should be between 8 feet and 10 feet long. Try different length rods to find the length rod that best matches your casting style. I like 8 1/2 foot rods, while most of my more intelligent and successful friends use 9-footers. But I am getting old and set in my outdated ways and do not like to listen to people anymore.

Reels

Choose a reel that has interchangeable spools or one that uses the newer cassette system. The ability to change a spool or cassette permits the use of fly lines with varying sink rates. This flexibility is very important in fishing the fly properly at the different depths of the lake. An alternative to interchangeable spools or cassettes is the use of shooting lines, which are 30-foot casting heads connected to a running line. These heads are interchangeable, so you do not need extra spools to add a different line to your inventory. Shooting lines take some practice getting accustomed to, as they have an extreme hinging effect between the shooting head and running line, which deadens the telegraphing of the strike from trout to rod.

Reels used for lake fishing must have a smooth, adjustable drag. Adjust the drag to its lightest setting, then tighten it just enough to keep it from over-spooling when you quickly strip off line. A drag set too tight may break the tippet under the combined resistance of a large trout and a long length of fly line cutting through the water. A properly adjusted drag will help protect your light tippet from trout that race off into the sunset.

Most fly lines are only 90 feet long, and larger trout can pull that amount of line off a reel more quickly than you might think. To handle these emergencies, a reel should be capable of holding 75 to 100 yards of backing. Because backing also fills the bottom of the spool, you reel up the fly line on a larger diameter for a faster retrieve. Use a good-quality braided-Dacron backing and secure it to the reel and fly line with reliable knots.

Fly Lines

The weight of the fly line must match the rod for the distance you intend to fish. Sound confusing? Generally, most rods are rated for the line weight that optimizes casting performance at 30 feet. This method works well for normal casting distances, but not for lake fishing, where you need to get as much distance out of the rod as possible. Thus you must fine-tune your rod with the line weight that will cast the farthest for you.

Most fly shops have demo lines of different weights that they will let you try out in order to determine the best one for your rod. Normally you want a weight forward line, which shoots line more easily than a double-taper type. Try a line that matches the rod's rated weight, and cast as far as you can while still maintaining control of the casting loop. You need this loop control to turn the leader and fly over and extend them beyond the fly line. Note the distance of the cast. Then try line weights smaller and larger. By testing these different lines at the distance needed for lake fishing, you'll be able to match your casting style and rod to a line weight that will give you the best distance with good loop control.

Fly lines come in a wide variety of colors. Sinking-line colors are often muted, while floating-line colors run from muted to intensely bright. A number of anglers have told me that brightly-colored lines will not spook fish any more than a muted color. I will not argue with them, but in my observations I have seen trout swim away from floating bright red, yellow, and orange fly lines and swim without alarm under less conspicuously colored ones. So I choose subdued colors for all of my lines. But whether bright or muted, any fly line flashing over fish will make them nervous or spook them. So try to keep your false casting to a minimum. If possible false-cast away from working fish; then on the last forward cast, change the direction to deliver the line to the desired spot.

The first line you buy should be a floating line, which will cover all of your surface fishing and some of the subsurface techniques. As you spend more time on lakes you will find the need to add an intermediate line or one of the new clear stillwater fly lines from Scientific Anglers. These lines are designed to sink slowly below the surface and keep flies fished shallow from dragging. That's right, dragging. The surface water on a lake is often moving in the direction of the wind, while the water inches below holds still. This surface movement will drag a floating line and sunken fly away from the area you are fishing. A slow-sinking intermediate line sinks below this surface movement, eliminating drag and giving you better line control when fishing a nymph close to the surface.

Controlling the depth at which you fish your fly is a basic requirement for lake fishing. This is accomplished by using a floating line and adding weight to the fly or by using a range of fly lines designed to sink at predetermined rates. An intermediate line is the slowest sinking of all, and the sink rate increases as you move to line Types I, II, III, IV, and V. The value of each number represents the approximate distance in inches that the line will sink in one second. Using these rating numbers, you can fish at any chosen depth by counting the number of seconds that a certain line is allowed to sink before you start fishing it back. For example, you want to fish your fly at 10 feet using a Type II sinking line.

You know this line sinks 2 inches per second, or 6 seconds per foot, so sinking 10 feet will take 60 seconds. The key is in matching the sink rate of the fly line to the depth you are fishing. You do not want to waste time waiting for a Type II line to sink 30 feet or struggle with a heavy Type IV line when you are trying to keep a nymph close to the surface on the retrieve.

Sinking lines come in a number of different designs. Sink-tip lines have a floating belly section and a sinking tip, which allows for easier line pick up between casts. Its disadvantage is the hinge in the line between the floating and sinking sections; this hinge inhibits a straight-line connection between you and the fly, which reduces sensitivity to a strike. Missing the delicate takes of a trout can be reduced by carefully watching the point at which the floating section enters the water and setting the hook at the first sign of any unusual movement.

Sink-tip lines work well for fishing over drop-offs and from the shore, where you do not want the belly of the line dragging the bottom in the shallow water. I also like using a sink-tip line when casting to a moving school of baitfish. This situation requires quick casts to an area, fishing them back in 10 feet or so, and then picking up the line to cast again. Fishing a sinking line under these conditions would overload the rod when lifting the submerged line from the water, unless you strip it in or roll cast it to the surface. The floating section of the sink-tip allows you to lift more line off the water without overloading the rod, giving a quicker pick-up with less disturbance to the water.

Full-sinking lines are designed to sink at the same rate along the whole length of the belly section (the thick middle of the fly line). But its rear running line and front tip section are thinner and sink at a slower rate. This difference in sink rates causes a hinging effect between the rod and the line and line-sag between the belly and leader. The hinging effect is not as great with the sink-tip lines, but it is there nonetheless.

You can reduce line sag between the rod and line by putting the tip of rod down into the water. To reduce line-sag between the line belly and fly, use a shorter leader and weighted fly, which permit the line tip and fly to sink at nearly the same rate as the fly line belly.

Uniform-sinking lines were designed to reduce the hinging problem and line-sag. Because the weight of the line is constant even throughout the small-diameter sections, the thin tip sinks at the same rate as the thicker belly, making a straighter line connection from the fly to the rod. If you keep your rod tip in the water on the retrieve, a uniform-sinking line is the most sensitive and responsive of all full-sinking lines.

Whatever types of sinking lines you use, try to have at least a Type II and IV, then add a III and V later. Rig the slow-sinking intermediate line with your surface-fishing rod since you will normally fish light tippets with it.

Some sinking lines mark the forward and rear portion by a change in color to help you determine, as you are retrieving, when to pick up the line for next cast. If you lift the rod too soon, you will pull it out of the fishing area and overload the rod, causing the line to collapse in a heap around you. If you strip the line in too far, you waste time false-casting the line back out. One way to eliminate this problem is to determine the distance at which you want to stop the retrieve and begin another cast, and then make a foot-long mark on your line with a waterproof marker. Unfortunately, such marks can be impossible to see when the light level is low. For a mark that's easier to detect, wrap a band of fly-tying thread about 1/3 of an inch wide on the line; whip finish and glue it. Then you will not even have to look for this mark; you will feel it as you strip in line between your pinched fingers.

To keep fly lines performing at their best, you must take care of them. Clean lines after each use and during midday fishing breaks. A smooth, dirt-free surface insures those extra feet of distance needed to cover far-off trout.

Leaders and Tippets

Leaders for surface fishing tend to be long—typically from 9 to 12 feet with 4 to 6 feet of tippet added to them. This combination can be downright miserable to cast even when the wind is not blowing, but a long leader is necessary to keep the fly line away from feeding trout. Normally the finer the tippet used, the longer your leader and tippet combination should be. Using a long fine tippet will help the fly float or drift properly and is less conspicuous to the trout than a heavier tippet.

Remember, leaders used while surface fishing must turn over and extend properly to keep the fly away from the fly line. A leader that collapses in a pile or tangles in the air will spook any trout it lands close to. Tapered knotless leaders with a tippet attached are best for surface fishing. They are designed to turn over properly, and the smooth, knotless surface will not catch weeds when a hooked trout bent on escaping cuts through a patch of vegetation.

A floating line with a long leader achieves the best imitation of insects emerging from the bottom. The long leader allows a small, lightly weighted fly to sink without the aid of added weight to the leader. To make a leader this long, use a 6- or 7-foot knotless leader and add enough tippet—anywhere from 5 to 20 feet—to reach the bottom. The finer the tippet, the faster the fly will sink.

Leaders for sinking lines are normally shorter and stronger than those used with floating lines. They can be as short as 4 feet or up to 10 feet and longer. Use shorter leaders with fast sinking lines. This combination allows the fly to stay level with the line as it sinks and as it's retrieved. Off-color water or heavy flies can also be fished with a short strong leader. Sinking lines require longer leaders in clear or shallow-water conditions since the added length keeps the line away from the fly. Moreover, smaller flies swim more naturally with a long, light leader.

In any given fishing situation, the size of the tippet depends on how large or small the fly is, how clear the water is, and how leader-shy the trout are. I like using 4X or 5X but will go as light as 7X or as heavy as 2X if conditions call for it.

Strike Indicators

Most anglers think a strike indicator is for river use only. But if you are fishing a lake with a floating line, a sunken fly, and a long leader, the only way you can detect delicate strikes without using a strike indicator is to watch the tip of the fly line. This can be difficult or impossible if you are wading deep and the fly line tip is 40 feet away. A strike indicator is considerably easier to see and also gives you the ability to adjust the fly's depth by moving the indicator up or down on the leader.

A high-floating dry fly with a nymph hanging below as a dropper is a good choice for fishing depths from one to fifteen feet. To fish a nymph at a certain depth, attach it to one end of a dropper tippet of the desired length; then tie the other end to the bend of the dry-fly hook. This system is simple to tie, and as long as you have a dry fly you will never be without an indicator. Since the flies are in line, the system casts well, and every once in a while a trout will smack the dry fly.

Poly yarn is another choice for use as an indicator. You can tie a small bunch on at the end of your leader with a clinch knot, and then tie the desired length of tippet on the leader behind the yarn. This places the tippet at a right angle to the leader.

Another way to use yarn as an indicator is to attach it to the leader or tippet with a slip knot. This allows you to change the fishing depth simply by moving the yarn; you need not add or remove tippet material.

Poly yarn floats better if it is fluffed up by combing it before installing it to the leader. Cut it to size after it is attached to the line, and then grease the yarn with a good floatant. Smaller indicators cast easier than larger ones, but if cut too small, they become difficult to see and may not float the nymph.

There are commercially made indicators that can also be used. Many are reusable and adjustable. They tend to be bulky, since most are designed more for use in rivers where long casts are not necessary. But there are a few streamlined ones that cast well and stay in place.

Droppers and Tailing Flies

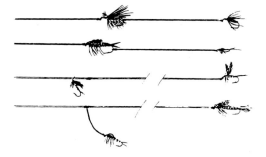

Dropper and tailing-fly techniques can be used with floating or sinking lines; in either case, match the flies to the fishing conditions and the hatches you want to imitate. Dropper is the name given to individual flies that are added up the leader at intervals of 2 feet or more from the end or "point" fly. Attach the dropper to the larger diameter tag-end of a blood knot. Keep the tag short, 2 or 3 inches, or it will tangle during the cast. You can also slide the fly onto the leader, and then tie a blood knot that is larger than the eye of the hook, which will keep the fly from sliding past the knot. An effective technique for imitating a midge pupa or nymph hanging in the surface film is to use a ring-eye hook as a sliding dropper and a floating fly at the point. The dropper will hang straight down, just as the naturals do, and the dry will act as a strike indicator.

A tailing fly follows or hangs below the point fly. To rig up a tailing fly, attach a length of tippet to the eye of the tailing fly. Then use a clinch knot to tie the other end of the tippet to either the bend or the eye of the point fly. The length of the tippet between the flies is determined by the distance you want to keep between them and the type of flies you are fishing—about 2 to 4 feet for sunken flies, 2 to 10 feet for floating ones.

The tailing fly technique allows you to use a lighter tippet on the smaller tailing fly. This tandem fly combination is less likely to tangle when casting or fishing. Using the tailing-fly method is handy when you want to swim a small nymph behind a larger wet fly. It can also be used to hang a small nymph or dry fly behind a larger, more visible dry fly, which acts as an indicator.

Lake-Fishing Techniques

Rising Trout

Surface-feeding trout can be the most exciting or most frustrating experience in lake fishing. It all depends upon how you approach them. If you charge in without any forethought, the trout will vanish. Big dividends await the angler who takes time to evaluate the situation. When fish are rising consistently and regularly, determining the type of rise will make the fly selection and presentation easier and more productive. Wearing polarized sunglasses will not only protect your eyes from errant flies and sun fatigue, but will aid in finding and analyzing rises. Use binoculars to take a closer look at floating insects and rises without disturbing the water by getting too close.

Rises are surface disturbances caused by trout feeding at the top of the water column. They may occur right at the surface or a few feet below. A fish feeding beneath the surface displaces the water above it, causing a bulge or a ring to form. If the fish is quite close to the top, a fin or part of the body may break the surface as the trout turns toward the bottom.

A surface rise appears when a trout takes an insect directly from or slightly beneath the surface film. A small, delicate sip rise that leaves an air bubble behind indicates that the trout is capturing food that is trapped in or sitting on the surface film and is unlikely to escape. These easily caught prey include spinners, emerging or crippled caddis, mayfly or midge, and terrestrials. Quick or hurried surface rises normally indicate trout are feeding on prey that is more likely to escape, such as adult caddis or mayflies.

Slow, deliberate, subsurface rises, signaled by a soft bulge or by a ring that leaves no air bubble, suggest trout are feeding on easily caught prey, such as midge pupa and mayfly emergers or nymphs. Violent or frenzied subsurface boils indicate trout are feeding on something larger or quicker that has a chance to escape—baitfish, leeches, and emerging caddis or mayflies.

Observing the riseform not only indicates what the trout is feeding on, but may also give information about the trout's feeding pattern and direction of travel. Unlike fish in rivers, which can wait for the current to deliver a meal, trout in lakes must cruise to find food. When a plentiful supply is available, trout settle into a feeding rhythm, traveling a set course that often forms an oval pattern. These patterns may occur on open water, follow the face of a cliff or shoreline, or center upon weed beds and foam lines. To avoid spooking the fish with your fly line, cast to the closest part of the oval circuit with enough lead-time to let the fly settle before the trout returns. Fishing a nymph pattern requires more lead-time since the fly must sink to the proper level before the fish arrives. If the feeding circuit is small, trout may be spooked by a random cast. Instead, when the fish surfaces, try to place your fly at the edge of the riseform closest to you. The surface disturbance from the rise will help hide the delivery of the fly, and when the trout turns to feed again, he will see it.

Sporadic rises are the most difficult to fish since you have no idea about what direction the trout is heading. All you can do is make an educated guess. Trout normally follow the edges of weed beds, shore lines and drop-offs. This tendency narrows your choice down in these areas, and you have about a 50 percent chance of being right. In open water with no indication of the trout's direction, pick a point 10 or 15 feet to the right or left of the last rise, and place your fly there. Lightly twitching the fly after it has settled may help draw the trout's attention to the fly if he is swimming away from it.

Searching the Water

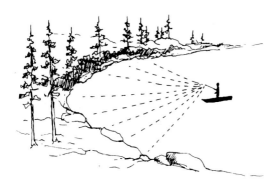

The sad truth for dry-fly purists is that trout in lakes feed on subsurface prey at least 90 percent of the time. Any angler expecting to catch them must deliver his offering down where the fish are feeding. You must choose a productive fly, the right locations, and the proper depth—all with little or no indication that trout are in the area. Under these circumstances, systematic searching casts are more productive than random casts, which often spook or fail to locate trout. The systematic searching of an area or depth may take more time, but you will cover all the water and give any trout there a look at the fly.

When systematically searching an area or depth, begin by fishing the water closest to you. After completing the first cast, place your next cast—with the same length of line—a short distance to one side. Successive casts should be placed at regular intervals in the direction you wish to be moving. The distance between casts varies with the clarity of the water. In clear water, where trout can see farther, space your casts farther apart; in murky water, space them closer together. Once you have covered the closer water, extend your casts out and repeat the search pattern.

Use this searching method with both sinking and float-ing lines. Sinking lines add another dimension. Unless you have a clue about how deep the fish are, you must also search for the depth where trout are holding. Search the shallowest water first, then let the fly sink deeper on each successive cast. To keep track of the depth you are fishing, count the number of seconds you allow the fly or line to sink. Once you find the depth trout are holding at concentrate on that depth.

Cast and Wait

The cast and wait technique is the simplest to execute but the hardest one to fish. It requires patience, patience, and more patience. Use this method when fish are sporadically working an area, but giving no indication about the direction of travel. If you attempt to cover each rise with repeated pick-ups and casts, you run the risk of alarming the trout. It's best to cast to the edge of the area where most of the rises are occurring, and then let the fly sit. Slowly take most of the slack out of the line, as this will enable you to lift the rod gently to tighten up on any trout that takes your fly. Leaving a fly unmoved for a few minutes will try one's patience, so you might twitch the fly lightly to imitate the feeble struggle of a dying insect. Then wait some more. After a couple of twitch-es and waiting periods, slowly strip the fly out of the feeding area and cast to a new spot.

The cast and wait method works best with a floating line and a fly that is resting on, in, or close to the surface film. If you cannot see the fly, then you must pay close attention to the tip of the fly line or add a dry fly to your leader as a strike indicator. Any movement of the line or indicator fly requires an immediate lifting of the rod to set the hook. Trout can take and reject surface and subsurface flies with so little disturbance that you may notice only a slight movement at the tip of the fly line or a twitch of the dry-fly indicator. I have lost my share of fish because my attention wandered at the wrong time.

This method will work for all floating flies, emergers, unweighted pupa imitations, and lightly weighted nymphs. By using the dropper or tailing-fly method you can fish 1 to 3 nymphs, pupa, or small dry flies below a visible dry fly.

Cast and Retrieve

Cast and retrieve is the technique used most often by lake anglers. Simply cast to the area you intend to fish and then retrieve the fly back. You can use any fly line with this method; just match the line type to the depth of water you want to fish. When using a floating line with a sinking fly, wait for the fly to sink to the desired depth before starting the retrieve. With a sinking line, you must wait for the line to pull the fly down to the proper depth. Count the number of seconds the fly or line sinks to keep track of the depth you are fishing.

The difference between using a floating line and a sinking line occurs during the retrieve. As you retrieve a floating line, the fly is lifted from the desired fishing depth as it is pulled up by the buoyant line. This rising action is desirable if you are trying to imitate an insect swimming toward the surface, but it's a drawback if your imitation is supposed to crawl along the bottom. A sinking line keeps the fly down at the desired depth for most of the retrieve and is effective fishing imitations of insects and other creatures that hold close to the bottom.

The trick with this method is in the retrieve. You must make the fly behave like the natural you are trying to imitate, imparting a lifelike action by stripping, pulling, or hand-twisting the line at various speeds, with or without pauses. For example, some nymphs swim in a 2-inch burst of speed, pause for 5 seconds, then dart again, repeating this action over and over. Other creatures may swim slowly for a foot or so, and then stop for 10 seconds before moving again. Still others scoot along with few pauses. Thus to animate a fly correctly, you must have some understanding of the actions of the food form you are imitating. The biggest mistake made with this method is retrieving too fast when imitating crawling or swimming insects.

Sink and Retrieve

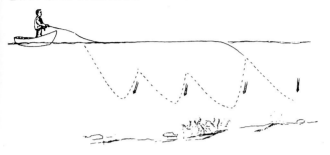

This is a version of the cast and retrieve method used to imitate an insect leaving the lake bottom and swimming to the surface. To execute this technique properly, use a floating fly line with a leader of 10 feet or longer. Cast and allow the fly to sink, keeping track of the depth by counting off the seconds as it sinks. This practice will allow you to return the fly to the exact depth at which you may have hooked a fish on an earlier cast, or to stop the sinking fly above a previously discovered weed bed. After the fly has reached the desired depth, retrieve it back to the surface imitating the speed and movement of the natural. Repeat the sink and retrieve at different depths until you have covered the area; then pick up and cast to a new spot.

When you are fishing in shallow water, or if you want the fly to sink only a short distance, apply fly floatant to the rear section of the leader, leaving untreated enough of the forward portion of the leader to reach the desired depth. The rear section of the leader will float, and the untreated front section will sink to the correct level. This is a deadly technique to use when trout are taking pupae or emergers that are rising to the surface.

Trout often take flies fished like this with little commotion. So if you are expecting to feel the strike at the rod, you will miss most of the takes. Watch where the floating line or leader enters the water. Any odd movement of the line or leader should be met with an immediate lifting of the rod to set the hook. Use a strike indicator if you are having difficulty seeing the strikes at the tip of the line. Many strikes occur during the pauses while retrieving the fly, so be extra vigilant then.

Lift and Settle

Many insects become more active prior to emergence. This activity often takes the form of false lift-offs from the bottom. Nymphs will rise a short distance and then settle back. Trout often cruise just above the nymphs' holding areas, feeding on them as they lift and drop.

The lift-and-settle method imitates this rise and fall motion and requires the use of a floating line to make the fly swim up properly. Cast to the fishing area, lower your rod tip to the water, and let the weighted fly settle to the bottom. Watch where the line enters the water or use a strike indicator, since trout will often hit as the fly is sinking. When the fly stops sinking, let it sit for 5 to 10 seconds, and then slowly lift your rod tip to imitate an insect leaving the bottom. Stop lifting when the rod tip is 2 to 4 feet above the water. After stopping the rod, lower it back to the water and strip in the slack line that develops as you drop the rod. Let the fly settle to the bottom and repeat the lifting and settling as you fish the fly back. Vary the height and speed of the lift as you fish out the cast.

Most strikes occur as the fly is settling to the bottom or just as it leaves the bottom. If a trout takes the fly as you lift the rod, it normally hooks itself on the tight line and you will feel it. The settling fly is a different matter. You will not feel the take, so watching the tip of the line or strike indicator is the key to successful hook-ups. Lift the rod at any unusual movement. If there is no resistance, drop the rod to let the fly settle and continue fishing.

Skating

Skating is a technique not often used, but under the right circumstances it can produce spectacular fishing. Some insects move across the surface of the water with the determination and grace of a college rowing team, while others struggle clumsily for a short distance and pause. Skating your fly over the surface of the water is the best way to imitate both of these behaviors.

Use a floating fly line with a long leader tied to a high-floating dry fly. I like to treat both the leader and fly with floatant to keep them from sinking. This treatment also makes the pick-up part of the cast easier and produces less disturbance on the water. Cast to the fishing area, dropping the tip of the rod to the water as the fly lands, and then pull in all the slack. With the rod tip down and pointing toward the fly, lift the rod and skate the fly back toward you. When the rod reaches vertical stop it, then drop it back toward the water while you take up the slack. Then repeat the action. The speed of the skating fly is controlled by how quickly you lift the rod tip; if you want more speed, strip in line as you lift the rod. The height you lift the rod determines the distance the fly skates. A short rod-lift produces a short skating distance; a long lift gives a long distance. Try to observe the action of the natural, and then imitate its behavior with your skating fly. When you are unable to determine the actions of the natural, vary the distance, speed, and pauses of the skated fly until you find the right combination.

With a strong wind at your back it may be possible to just lift and lower the rod as you move it over the area you are fishing. The wind will pick the fly up and bounce it around like a natural when you lift the rod. Dropping the rod will cause the fly to settle back on the surface. Repeat the lift, move, and drop of the rod through the area you are fishing. This is actually a form of dapping, but by moving the tip of the rod right or left as it's lifted, you cause the fly to skate across the surface in the direction of the rod movement.

Violent strikes occur when using this method, so adjust the tippet accordingly—to 3X, 4X, or 5X, depending on the size of the fish.

Wind Drifting

Any time there is wind blowing and you are on the move from one fishing area to another, you can use this technique. It is also helpful in locating trout when you must cover a large area. Both floating and sinking lines work with this method.

Wind drifting requires a boat or float tube. Move upwind of the water you want to fish, and position your craft to maintain a slow drift through the area. If the drift is too fast with the boat pointed into the wind, drag a sea anchor or bucket in the water from a rope tied to the front of the boat. This will help slow down your drift. Maintaining the proper speed while drifting in a boat is often troublesome, but it is important, and you will catch few trout if you ignore it. A float tube will not catch the wind as a boat does, and it's much easier to adjust the speed of the drift with an occasional kick of the fins.

Cast your line out at a right angle from your floating device. The object is to have your fly line and fly move at the same speed you are drifting. If your floating speed does not match that of the fly line, you will have to mend the line to get the best possible drag free drift. To call a trout's attention to the fly, twitch it occasionally during the drift.

Try to set up your drift so that you travel over areas with good fishing potential—the water around weed beds, edges of drop-offs, cliffs, rocky shore lines, and old river channels. After hooking a trout, mark the area and drift through it again or anchor close by and search it by casting.

Trolling

Trolling is a very productive way to explore new lakes when using a boat or float tube. It is by far the most relaxing and easiest method if you are new to fly fishing or if you just want to take it easy while you fish. Select a floating or sinking fly line that will fish at the desired depth. Then put on a fly to imitate a creature that spends a lot of time on the go, like a minnow, leech, or dragonfly nymph. Start fishing by casting or feeding line out as you move your craft in the direction you want to fish.

Gas or electric motors have their uses, but trolling a fly is not one of them. Insects and baitfish do not move at the steady pace of a motor-trolled fly. They swim slowly, pause a bit, and swim a little more. The slow speeds, pauses, and erratic actions of a trolled fly are best imitated from a rowed boat or a fin-powered float tube. The slow pull of an oar or kick of a fin, with a pause between each motion, imitates the natural action of nymphs, leeches, and baitfish. Trout have a hard time resisting a slowly-trolled fly. But do not get in the rut of only trolling one particular way. Change your speed, the distance between pauses, the length of pauses, and the amount of line trolled until you find the combination that works for the fish.

The length of fly line between you and the trolled fly is often dictated by the depth and clarity of the water. More trolled line allows the fly to sink deeper and distances it from the angler, but detecting a strike or setting the hook in a trout becomes increasingly difficult as you lengthen the line. Try to use the shortest line possible to reach the depth you want and to avoid spooking the trout.

Chapter 3

Caddisflies

(Order: Trichoptera)

The tent-shaped wings of the adult caddisfly are covered with fine hairs that give this order of insect its name—Trichoptera (Tricos=hair, Optera=wing). A caddisfly's life cycle normally takes one year, but can last as long as two years or as little as six months. The insect passes through four stages of development (egg, larva, pupa, and adult), a process called "complete metamorphosis." Caddisflies spend most of their lives in the larval stage. The larvae go through five instars, the intervals between molts, which must occur for growth. At the end of the final instar, the larvae build cocoons, and pupation is normally completed within two to four weeks. At the end of pupation, the pupae, correctly called "pharate adults," leave the cocoon and swim to the surface where the pupal shucks split open and the adults fly off the water. Adult caddisflies survive for one to four weeks. In that time they mate, and the females return to the water to deposit their eggs, which hatch in two to four weeks.

North America has 21 families, 145 genera and over 1,200 species of caddis—an impractical number to try to identify—and this overwhelming variety is probably the reason that caddisflies have always taken a back seat to the less abundant and more easily recognized mayflies. To aid in identification, caddisflies are categorized into five groups based on the type of larval retreat it makes, the type of case it builds, or the absence of a case altogether. These groups are: (1) free-living forms, (2) saddle-case makers, (3) purse-case makers, (4) net-spinners or retreat-makers, and (5) tube-case makers. Cases, or the lack of them, determine the caddisflies' habits and habitats.

The larvae of tube-case makers are more mobile than the other case makers. Moreover, by undulating their abdomens they force water through the tube cases and extract the oxygen—a way of "breathing" that is impossible for uncased caddis. These two characteristics make this group of caddisflies the most abundant type in the still waters of lakes and ponds. There are eight families of caddisflies in the tube-case maker group, and three of them, which are covered in the following pages, produce the most important hatches in lakes. Trout feed on all forms—larvae, pupae, and adults—as they become available. The fly angler who chooses the correct form to fish at the right time, place, and depth will have the satisfaction of hooking many trout.

Identifying caddisflies can be difficult. Trying to key a caddisfly past the Family level to Genus and specie is best left to biologists. Most of the information that a fly angler needs in order to choose the right fly and method of presentation can be gathered from understanding the habitats, habits, and characteristics of caddisflies at the Family level. The easiest form of the caddisfly to identify is the larva. The case or shelter the larva builds is often distinctive for each Family of caddisfly, though even within Families there can be differences in case shape, size, and materials of construction. Pupae and adult caddisflies are very difficult to key, but they do provide valuable information about the size and color of an appropriate imitation. To find out more about their underwater behavior, collect the caddisfly in its larval stage, which is the easiest to capture and identify. Then match its general case shape, size, and construction characteristics as closely as possible to one of the three major stillwater caddis larvae on the following pages.

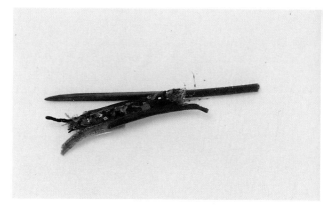

Longhorned Case Maker—Larva

Family: Leptoceridae   Size: 7-15 mm
Common Names: Black Dancer, Long-Horn Sedge, White Miller
Notice: Long antennae; may have long hind legs that project
    forward
J F M A M J J A S O N D E, M, W

    The cases of this family of caddisflies vary, but most are long
and slender. Depending on the genus and the available material,
cases may be constructed of plant fragments, silk, or small rocks
with twigs or conifer needles that extend past the ends of the case.
One genus, *Leptocerus* (**E**, **M**), includes a species that spins a silk
case and uses its long hind legs to swim about in aquatic vegetation. Black Dancer (**E**, **M**, **W**) cases are a rough tube made up of
small rocks with twigs and needles attached to the outside These
larvae are often seen crawling along the bottom and feeding.
Long-Horn Sedge (**E**, **M**, **W**) cases are slightly curved, often
tapered tubes of rock or plant fragments. These larvae are predators that roam the bottom in search of prey. White Miller (**E**, **M**, **W**)
cases are long and slender and made from rocks or bits of vegetation. The larvae climb and swim among weeds while feeding.

LaFontaine Cased Caddis (Light or Dark), Drifting Cased Caddis, Herl Nymph
Hook Size: 8-16

Search the weed beds and bottom for larvae of the Longhorned Case Makers. The family is very diverse, and you will not be able to choose the right fly or method of fishing it without first knowing what to imitate. Cases built from stones indicate that larvae spend most of their time on the bottom. Match a weighted fly to the color and size of the natural. Use a sinking or sink-tip line to keep the fly on the bottom as you fish it back with the cast and retrieve method. These bottom dwellers are not fast movers, so keep the retrieve slow. Since trout take these flies with little commotion, be quick to set the hook. If the caddisfly you captured has a case made from plant material, drop it back into the water and observe its motion. If the fly sinks, use the previous method; if it swims, choose a lightly weighted pattern that matches the natural. These larvae are slow, erratic swimmers that spend most of their time in and around weed beds. The depth of these beds will determine the type of fly line you need. Use the cast and retrieve method, retrieving the fly just fast enough to keep it out of the weeds while adding short pauses. Lift your rod to set the hook at the first sign of resistance. If there is no resistance, drop your rod tip and continue fishing. Check for weeds on the hook after you have fished out the retrieve.

Longhorned Case Maker—Pupa

Family: Leptoceridae   **Size: 7-15 mm**
Common Names: Black Dancer, Long-Horn Sedge, White Miller
Body Color: Black, brown or white
Notice: Long antennae coiled around base of abdomen
J F M A M J J A S O N D   E, M, W

On reaching maturity leptocerid larvae attach their cases to surfaces of submerged objects. They then seal off their cases and begin pupating. Pupation normally takes from two to four weeks. After the pupae have reach maturity they cut through the closed case and leave. These emerging pupae—called pharate adults—either crawl or swim to the surface. These hatches, which can be very intense for an hour or two, generally occur at dawn or dusk during the warmer months, shifting to daylight hours during the cooler spring and fall months. The emergence may last from two or three weeks or two or three months. Black Dancer (**E, M, W**) pupae emerge all summer and tend to swim and crawl out of the water during the first hours of daylight. Long-Horn Sedges (**E, M, W**) emerge by swimming to the surface. Their emergence runs from May through October with two- to three-week peak periods. White Millers (**E, M, W**) emerge by swimming to the surface after dark during the summer months.

Black Sparkle Pupa,
Brown Emergent Sparkle Pupa, White Miller

Hook Size: 8-16

There is no doubt that when these caddisflies emerge during the peak of a hatch, trout feed voraciously on the large numbers of emerging insects, often producing deep boils on the surface. The adults' long antennae make this caddis family easy to identify. The color and size of the adult will be your main clue for choosing the correct pupa imitation, time, and method to fish. Look for Black Dancer adults in the cool morning hours resting on vegetation along the shore, or gathering in mating swarms along the margins of lakes as the day warms. These pupae generally crawl out of the water to emerge during the early morning hours. Fish with a Black Sparkle Pupa at this time using the cast and retrieve method. Fish the deeper waters next to floating or emerging vegetation; when the imitation is close to the bottom, retrieve it slowly. Long-Horn Sedges emerge in a lake's shallow margins. Hatch times vary with the season. Any time you notice this adult caddisfly and trout are working close to the surface, fish a Brown Emergent Sparkle Pupa that matches the size of the adult. Use a floating line with the sink and retrieve method. Cast toward feeding trout; let the fly sink and then retrieve it back to the surface. Vary the depth of the fly and the speed of retrieve until you have fished out the cast or until you connect with a trout. White Millers emerge in the dark hours of night. Fish its imitation with a floating or sink-tip line retrieved slowly back along the edges of the lake.

Longhorned Case Maker—Adult

Family: Leptoceridae   **Size:** 7-15 mm
Common Names: Black Dancer, Long-Horn Sedge, White Miller
Body Color: Brown, green, yellow or white
Wing Color: Black, brown, straw yellow, or white
Notice: Long antennae
J F M A M J J A S O N D   E, M, W

Black Dancer (**E**, **M**, **W**) and Long-Horn Sedge (**E**, **M**, **W**) adults
from this caddisfly family perform their mating-swarm flights during
daylight hours. Like mayfly spinners, caddisflies in these swarms often
fly in an up-and-down pattern at the height of shoreline vegetation.
Black Dancers emerge by crawling out of the water, so the adults are
normally not available to trout during the hatch. The Long-Horn Sedge
adult, however, is available to trout as it emerges. But trout will take
adults of both types when the females return to deposit their eggs by
diving into the water, usually during the morning and evening hours.
This hatch provides anglers with superb dry-fly fishing for a good part
of the summer. White Millers (**E**, **M**, **W**) are most active in the hours
between sunset and sunrise through the warm summer months, when
emergence takes place and when females dive beneath water to lay
eggs. Discovering good numbers of spent White Millers in the shallows in the morning indicates that a hatch or egg-laying flight occurred
the previous night. The longevity and intensity of the Longhorned
Case Makers hatch make the adults of this caddisfly more available to
trout than caddis of any other family.

Deer Hair Caddis, Diving Caddis, Parkany Deer Hair Caddis—White

Hook Size: 10-16

The mating flights of the Black Dancers and Long-Horn Sedges indicate that egg-laden females will soon be hitting the water and diving under to lay their eggs. If you notice fish working on the surface at this time, there is a good chance that they are taking adults that have been blowing into the water or early egg layers. Tie on a Deer Hair Caddis or similar low water pattern that will closely match the natural and cast it toward the working trout. Let the fly sit a bit, then give it a light twitch to imitate a struggling caddisfly. Trout working under the surface may be feeding on either emerging caddis or egg-laying females. Identify the flying caddis. If they are Black Dancers, the trout are probably feeding on adult females, since Black Dancer pupae do not swim to the surface to emerge. But for Long-Horn Sedges, emergence and egg laying may occur at the same time. Start with a Diving Caddis the size and color of the natural. If the trout refuse your offering, then try an Emerging Caddis Pupa pattern. Use a floating or intermediate line with the cast and retrieve method. Mix the retrieve—slow or fast with pauses—until you find the right combination. White Miller adults appear after sunset, so you will be fishing more by sound and feel than by sight. Cast a good floating pattern like a Parkany Deer Hair Caddis in the direction of any surface disturbance. Immediately take two quick strips to remove the slack, and let the fly rest a short time. Then twitch the fly and repeat the cycle. This fishing is not for light tippets or faint-hearted fishermen.

Northern Case Maker—Larva

Family: Limnephilidae   **Size:** 18-25 mm
Common Name: Summer Flier Sedge, Late Summer Sedge
Notice: Cases made of small rocks, pieces of wood or plants
J F M A M J J A S O N D   E, M, W

This family of caddisflies has more species than any other in North America. Many of these caddisflies do not live in still water. Those that do are an important food source for trout in most lakes. Caddisflies in this family range in size from 6-30 mm. It is beyond the scope of this book to cover all the stillwater caddis of this group, but the larger members of this group, such as the Summer Flier Sedges (**E**, **M**, **W**) and Great Late Summer Sedges (**E**, **W**), are worth noting. These two large cased caddisflies are crawlers that cannot swim. Their cases, usually made from plant material, are relatively light, allowing these caddisflies to crawl around the weed beds that provide their food and shelter. These caddisflies winter over in deep water, then migrate to the weedy margins of the lake after ice-out. Hungry trout wait to intercept them at this time.

Hazel's Cased Caddis,
Cased Caddis, Medium Cased Caddis,

Hook Size: 6-10, 3X Long

The Summer Flier Sedge and Great Late Summer Sedge are available to trout from ice-out or early spring to late summer. At ice-out they migrate from deeper water to the weedy margins of the lake. Trout cruise the edges of weed beds and drop-offs hunting these migrators. They pick cased caddisflies off the bottom and eat the case along with the larva. These larvae crawl along the bottom, and to imitate them your fly must be on the bottom as well. Use a sinking line to get the fly down and keep it there during the retrieve. Holding your rod tip in the water, retrieve the fly at a slow, steady pace. Trout may take these imitations gently or violently, so lift the rod to set the hook at the slightest pause. Later in the spring, after these cased larvae have moved into the weeds, fish the outer edges of weed beds or just above the vegetation. Fishing these weedy shallow areas requires a sinking, sink-tip or a floating line with a weighted fly that will reach to bottom. Do not use too heavy a combination or you will constantly hang up on the weeds during the slow retrieve. On reaching maturity these larvae pupate for up to two months. From mid to late summer, you may find the large, sealed cases of pupating caddis among the weed beds. Trout may still take a cased larva imitation, but probably not as readily as they did when the larvae were active.

Northern Case Maker—Pupa

Family: Limnephilidae   **Size: 14-24 mm**
Common Name: Summer Flier Sedge, Late Summer Sedge
Body Color: Ginger to brown
J F M A M J J A S O N D   E, M, W

Summer Flier Sedge (**E, M, W**) and Late Summer Sedge (**E, W**) larvae live and feed in the weed beds of lakes. Once mature, these larvae attach their cases to underwater objects and close the case openings. This is the start of pupation, which takes up to eight weeks for these large caddisflies. Fully-developed pupae leave their cases and swim steadily to the surface, where their pupal shucks split open and the adults emerge. On reaching the surface, some pupae may continue to swim until they reach surface weeds or the shore. These hatches normally occur for an hour or two, any time from late morning to late evening, but during warmer months expect more evening hatches. Summer Flier Sedges generally emerge from July to September and Late Summer Sedges from August to November. These emergent caddisflies often have a two- to three-week peak of activity on most lakes. Trout feed actively on these fast-moving emergers from the time they leave their cases until they emerge and fly off as adults.

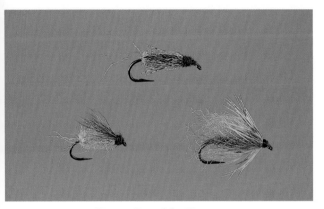

Deep Sparkle Pupa, Emergent Sparkle Pupa, Sparkle Caddis Pupa

Hook Size: 6-10, 2X Long

Large caddisflies clinging to shoreside vegetation or flying out over the water indicate a recent hatch. Search among submerged weeds for large caddis cases. When you find a closed one carefully peel it open and match your imitation to the color and size of the pupa. If you are unable to find a pupa, capture an adult and use the size and coloration of wing and body for your example. These pupae swim by rapidly paddling their legs, which gives them a steady pulsating forward motion. Use a floating line with the sink and retrieve method. Add slight, but continuous, twitches of the rod tip during the retrieve to imitate the swimming action of the pupa as it rises. A pupa imitation is effective during the hatch or as a searching pattern before or after a hatch. Once trout turn on to these large caddisflies, they will hit a properly fished fly even when no naturals are emerging. Emerging pupae are targets for trout from the moment they leave the bottom until they fly off as adults. At the beginning of the hatch, most takes will come close to the bottom. As the hatch progresses, trout will follow the pupae to the surface, so fish a lightly weighted pupa imitation closer to the surface. Trout take these escaping naturals and imitations aggressively. Set the hook gently so you do not break off the fish.

Northern Case Maker—Adult

Family: Limnephilidae   **Size:** 14-24 mm
Common Names: Summer Flier Sedge, Late Summer Sedge
Body Color: Ginger to brown
Wing Color: Ginger to brown
J F M A M J J A S O N D   E, M, W

The large adult caddisflies of Summer Flier Sedges (**E, M, W**) and the Late Summer Sedges (**E, W**) normally emerge from their pupal shuck in open water above weedy areas. Some pupae hit the surface swimming hard and continue paddling across the surface toward the shore to emerge. Most of these newly-hatched adult caddisflies spend little time on the water before flying off. During hatches, trout often feed more on pupae as they swim to the surface than the emerged adults. Adult caddisflies live for a week or two, and to keep from dehydrating they fly out and touch the water to collect a drink. During the peak of a hatch there are often good numbers of adult caddisflies returning for a drink throughout the day. Adults mate while hiding on shoreside foliage. Egg-laden females return to open water and deposit their eggs on the surface either by gently touching it or crashing into it. Some sit quietly on the surface while others touch and go. It is during the females' egg-laying flights—often occurring in the calm morning or evening hours—that trout see the largest concentrations of these caddisflies.

Canoe Fly,
Deer Hair Caddis, Elk Hair Caddis

Hook Size: 4-10

It's hard not to notice these caddis when they are flying, but it is difficult to catch them in flight without a big insect net. Instead of trying to capture them on the wing, watch where they land on shoreside vegetation and catch them there. Match your imitation to the size and color of the natural. During the day, trout often follow adult caddisflies that return to the water to drink, and as the flies dip to the water's surface trout try to catch them. More caddisflies end up in the water on windy days. When these adults are flying, sporadic, splashy trout rises can offer some exciting fishing. Cast your dry fly close to the last rise. Let the fly sit for a few seconds; then lightly twitch it a couple of times and let it rest again. Trout often take the fly as it lands on the water or after the first twitches, so be ready. As female caddisflies return to the open water to lay their eggs, trout begin feeding on them. Position yourself within casting distance of the feeding trout. Cover the close water first, and then extend your casts. The twitch and pause method best imitates the actions of a caddisfly struggling in the surface. Use a low-water pattern like the Canoe Fly to imitate spent flies and the higher riding Deer Hair or Elk Hair Caddis patterns for caddisflies that are more active on the surface.

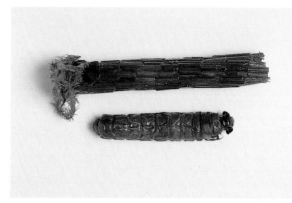

Giant Case Maker—Larva

Family: Phryganeidae   Size: 20-40 mm
Common Names: Traveling Sedge, Rush Sedge
Body Color: Pale yellow to light tan
Notice: Cases spirally tapered cylinders of plant materials
J F M A M J J A S O N D   E, M, W

Traveling and Rush Sedge larvae are herbivores during their early instars and become predators in their last instars. For concealment while crawling in and among weeds, they build their cases from pieces of leaves or wood in continuous rings or winding spirals. These cases offer the larvae no protection from feeding trout that will eat the case along with the larvae. If disturbed these larvae can abandon their cases and swim for safety. Submerged weed beds in the margins of lakes are their preferred habitat. They spend most of their early larval instars buried deep within the weeds, giving trout few chances at them. As the larvae grow and enter the predator stage of their last instars, concealment becomes increasingly more difficult when they move around in search of prey. Movement by any of these large larvae while close to the edge of a weed bed puts them in jeopardy of being rooted out by a hungry trout. At maturity these larvae attach their cases to submerged objects and close off its ends. They spend the next six to eight weeks pupating, which makes them unavailable to trout until the pupae emerge.

Lake Peeking Caddis, Hazel's Cased Caddis, Caddis Larva

Hook Sizes: 4-10, 3X Long

These cased caddisfly larvae live among submerged weeds. They make their cases from available plant materials. Collect a larva and match your imitation to the size and color of the case. Also note the color and size of the larvae. A closed case indicates these larvae are pupating and not crawling about searching for food. Fishing a larva imitation at a time when few larvae are moving may prove unproductive. In the spring, as submerged weeds are spreading with new growth, trout prowl among the sparse foliage in search of prey. Giant Case Makers are large enough at this time of the season to catch a trout's attention, particularly if the larvae are moving about. Use a sinking or sink-tip line to keep the fly close to the bottom. Attach a weighted case imitation and fish a searching pattern around weedy areas using the cast and retrieve method. Remember these cased larvae are crawlers, so creep the imitation along the bottom. As the season progresses and the weed beds become denser, fish their outer edges or just above them. The takes are often subtle, so lift your rod to set the hook at the first sign of resistance. If you discover large populations of these larvae in the lake, try using an uncased larva imitation that matches the natural. These uncased larvae are swimmers; to imitate them, vary the speed of the retrieve and add short pauses. Hungry trout will not pass up such a large morsel.

Giant Case Maker—Pupa

Family: Phryganeidae   Size: 15-30 mm
Common Names: Traveling Sedge, Rush Sedge
Body Color: Browns, grays, greens, or yellows
J F M A M J J A S O N D   E, M, W

On reaching maturity the larvae from this family attach their cases to submerged objects in the weedy areas or burrow into silty bottoms of the lake. Then they seal their cases and begin pupation. The change from larvae to pupa takes six to eight weeks for these large caddisflies. When ready to emerge, the fully developed pupae chew open their cases and crawl out. While still enveloped in their pupal shucks, they crawl or swim off with a pair of long, oar-like legs. Traveling Sedge pupae can emerge from midday until after sunset in open water. Rush Sedge pupae move by crawling or swimming into the shallows and then crawl out onto shoreside vegetation to emerge. Their emergence times vary but tend to be later in the day, sometimes occurring after dark. These pupae are in constant peril from the time they leave the security of their anchored cases until emergence. The open-water or shoreward migration by these large pupae triggers an immediate response from trout that feed heavily on these easily caught pupae.

Sedge Pupa,
Deep Sparkle Pupa, Sparkle Caddis Pupa

Hook Size: 4-10, 2X Long

The first sign of adult Traveling Sedges running across the water's surface indicates the start of an emergence, which generally occurs in the late morning. Try to capture one of the emerging pupae or newly-hatched adults and match your pupa imitation to the size and color of the natural. Tie on a pupa imitation. Do not be tempted to put on a dry fly even though you see a few splashy rises for below the surface trout are often feeding heavily on swimming pupae. Use the sink and retrieve method with a floating line, long leader and weighted fly. Cast toward working fish and let the fly settle, varying the depth on each cast, and then retrieve your imitation back to the surface. Retrieve the fly at different speeds while lightly twitching or vibrating the tip of your rod. The floating line will cause the fly to rise to the surface like the natural, and trout are likely to hit the fly at any time during the retrieve. Rush Sedges found on shoreside brush is your signal to fish a pupa imitation the size and color of the adult. These pupae migrate from weedy areas to the shore from late afternoon until dark or after. To copy their migration use the cast and retrieve method with a sink-tip or floating line. Cast your fly from the shore to deeper water. Let the fly settle close to the bottom, then begin the retrieve. These pupae may be crawling or swimming, so vary the retrieve until a trout grabs your fly.

Giant Case Maker—Adult

Family: Phryganeidae Size: 15-30 mm
Common Names: Traveling Sedge, Rush Sedge
Body Color: Browns, grays, greens or yellows
Wings: Generally patterned browns, grays or yellows
J F M A M J J A S O N D   E, M, W

When Traveling Sedge pupae reach the surface, they often
hang quietly in the surface film. After a short time the pupal
shucks split open and the adults push themselves out of their
confining shucks. They take off, traveling like miniature motor
boats across the surface. These are large caddisflies, and their
late-morning to mid-afternoon emergences are often visible to
anglers and trout from long distances on calm days. During
evening hours, egg-laden female Traveling Sedges fly out and
land on the water to deposit their eggs. After completing the
task, they scurry or fly off to safety. Rush Sedge adults—named
for the lakeside rushes they rest on—generally are not available
to trout until they begin depositing their eggs in the evening. The
female caddisflies dive into the water from a good height and
swim to protected, submerged positions to lay their eggs.
Afterward they swim back to the surface to skitter across the
water or fly off. The commotion caused by these caddisflies hitting and leaving the water gets the attention of every trout in the
area and invites them to feed on diving, swimming, or traveling
sedges.

Traveling Sedge,
Tom Thumb, Diving Caddis

Hook Size: 4-10, 2X Long

Traveling Sedge pupae often rest quietly on the surface a few moments before the adults begin to emerge. After emerging, the adults also pause a few more moments before they start traveling. Patterns such as a Tom Thumb—matched to the body color and size of the natural—can be used to imitate the emerging adults with raised wings and trailing pupal shuck. With a floating line and floatant-treated leader, cast the fly toward feeding trout. After the fly lands, let it sit a few moments, and then use the skating method to skitter the fly across the surface, copying the speed of the natural. A Traveling Sedge or similar fly pattern matching the size and color of the adult imitates the natural coming back to lay her eggs. Cast the fly toward working trout and let it rest a few moments; then skate it a short distance and repeat the cycle. A Traveling Sedge pattern imitates the adults hitting or skittering across the surface. Twitching and skating the fly often results in explosive strikes from frenzied trout. Rush Sedge adults are normally available to trout only as they return to lay their eggs. They dive bomb the water's surface like miniature kamikaze pilots, swim under the water to lay their eggs, and then return to the surface to skitter or fly off. Match your fly to the adult's size and color. Use the Diving Caddis with the sink and retrieve method to imitate the swimming adults.

Chapter 4

Mayflies

(Order: Ephemeroptera)

As their wings catch the wind and they sail across the water, mayfly adults resemble delicate miniature sailboats. Most anglers regard them as the most beautiful of all aquatic insects. Unlike caddis, they undergo an incomplete metamorphosis, passing through only three stages of development: egg, nymph, and adult. Mayflies spend most of their lives—a year, three at most—underwater in the nymphal stage and on reaching maturity, nymphs with fully developed darkened wing pads leave their aquatic environment for a terrestrial one as an adult. This transformation, referred to as a "hatch," normally occurs at certain times of the day with large numbers of emerging adults involved. A hatch may last an hour or two each day and continue for up to several weeks. Mayfly adults have two phases. Those in the first stage are called duns or subimagos, which are the insects that emerge from the nymphs. Within a day or two after emerging, duns molt by shedding their exoskeleton, and the second phase—called spinners or imagos—begins. These spinners are nonfeeding—their sole purpose is to reproduce, which they accomplish by swarming, mating, and then laying their eggs. The swarming flights, often seen around margins of lakes, are made up of male mayflies. These very distinctive up-and-down or spinning flight-patterns give spinners their name. Any female that flies into a swarm is clasped from below by a male; then flying together, they mate. Later, females return to the water to lay their eggs and often end up exhausted or spent on the water. These occurrences are called "spinner falls." Spinners' lives are short, varying from a few hours to a few days. This is probably the reason that their scientific name is Ephemeroptera; the definition of ephemeral is "lasting for a markedly brief time."

Based on the behavioral characteristics of the nymphs, mayflies are divided into four groups: swimmers, burrowers, crawlers, and clingers with only the first three of importance to lake fly fishers. Nymphs are the easiest stage to identify, and by observing their characteristics you should be able to place them easily into their correct group and family. North America has a total of 18 mayfly families, and four of these make up most of the major stillwater hatches. Inlets and outlets often have other mayfly families that live in moving water, and they are not covered in this book. Information about these mayflies should be available in one of the listed references.

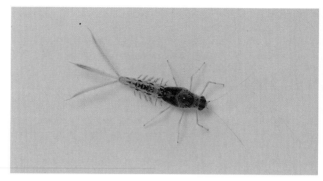

Speckle-wing Quill—Nymph

Family: Baetidae   Size: 6-12 mm
Genus: *Callibaetis*
Body Color: Light grays, tans, or pale greens
Notice: Antennae longer than twice the head width
J F M A M J J A S O N D   E, M, W

Callibaetis mayflies are widespread across North America, but they are of greatest importance in the West, where they appear in nearly all stillwaters containing trout. These nymphs are swimmers, often darting about in three- to six-inch bursts. The long antennae on these nymphs separate them from the other mayfly swimmers, which is important to remember because they behave and emerge differently than other stillwater nymphs. This is a multi-brood family, often having two or three generations a year depending on the number of warm months in a given locale. These nymphs grow rapidly, feeding on algae growths that cover plant surfaces. Under ideal conditions, they go from hatched egg to mature nymph in six weeks. They spend their lives in shallow weedy areas of a lake's margins. As mayfly nymphs approach maturity their wing pads darken. Just before emerging, *Callibaetis* nymphs swim up out of the weeds and then settle again repeatedly until they finally swim all the way to the surface and emerge. Emergence lasts for an hour or two. Starting times vary from mid-morning in the warmer months to mid-afternoon during cooler months. Trout focus their complete attention on these easily caught nymphs as soon as the insects leave the shelter of weeds.

CDC *Callibaetis* Floating Nymph/Emerger, Timberline, Marabou P.T. Nymph
Hook Size: 12-16

These mayfly nymphs inhabit weedy shallows, often in very dense populations. Cruising trout often feed on any errant nymphs leaving the protective weed cover, but most of these nymphs are safe from trout until they begin to emerge. Their rising and falling during pre-emergence, and then their final ascent, attract trout to the shallows, where they cruise over and around weedy areas with increasing anticipation hours before a hatch begins. The lift-and-settle method mimics the pre-hatch rising and falling of the natural. Use it an hour or two before the hatch starts. Vary the steady lifting of the rod by slightly twitching or vibrating the rod tip as you lift it to impart a swimming motion on the fly. Change to the sink and retrieve method as the hatch progresses and nymphs start heading for the surface. This becomes evident when you begin to notice boils from subsurface feeding trout. Alter the speed of the retrieve, and try it both with and without the slight rod-tip action. At times, slow steady retrieves without any pauses or actions work best. Trout often become very selective and key more to the action of the fly than the pattern, so it is important to vary the retrieve until you find the right combination. It pays to have a floating nymph pattern for those cold, rainy days when nymphs spend more time in the surface film trying to emerge and trout key on them there. Use the cast and wait method with or without an indicator. Twitch the fly slightly every so often to call a trout's attention to it.

Speckle-wing Quill—Dun

Family: Baetidae   Size: 6-12 mm
Genus: *Callibaetis*
Body Color: Top, brownish olives to grays; bottom, light tan to olive
Notice: Mottled wings and small hind wings
J F M A M J J A S O N D   E, M, W

The speckled wings on these duns make them easy to identify. Each year they have multi-generations, which cause definite
peak hatch periods that generally occur in late spring, then again
in early- to mid-summer and finally in the fall. These generational
peak-periods have gradual beginnings and endings that often
overlap with one another, causing an almost constant hatch
throughout the season. Early-season hatched duns are normally
two hook sizes larger than duns in autumn hatches. Emergence
time and duration vary with the season and weather. Generally
hatches occur from mid-morning to mid-afternoon. During cooler
months they are often an hour or two later than those occurring
during the warmer months. Hatches occurring on overcast or
rainy days can last up to four hours, while on sunny days they
may last only one hour. On cool overcast days, emerging duns
spend longer times on the surface, but on sunny days they emerge
and fly off quickly. The length and consistency of this hatch make
it a favorite of both trout and dry-fly anglers.

Callibaetis Comparadun, Speckle-wing Parachute, Natural Dun *Callibaetis*

Hook Size: 12-18

These mayflies emerge in open water above submerged weed beds, often in or near shallow water. Choose a casting position that will allow you to cover the weedy area without putting yourself between the submerged weeds and deeper water. This reduces the possibility of spooking incoming trout. Trout normally concentrate on the nymphs at the start of these hatches; if you notice *Callibaetis* duns on the surface that are getting no attention from trout, use a nymph pattern and get it down to where the trout are feeding. Put on your favorite dry fly only after trout start surfacing to feed on emerging or floating duns. Match your imitation to the size and color of the natural. Remember, trout see the dun from below so match the dun's underside color. Trout can be very discerning when feeding on the surface. Successful hook-ups are the result of minimizing the effects of anything that may alert trout to the forgery. Make your leader long and fine. Then use a Comparadun or parachute pattern that floats flush on the surface. Both present a more realistic impression to trout than a hackle pattern resting on a lake's flat surface. Cast your fly close to the rising trout then employ the cast and wait method with an occasional light twitch to the fly. If the fly is resting among feeding trout, this method will produce many more hook-ups than trying to cover all the rises with repeated casts, which often spooks the trout.

Speckle-wing Quill—Spinner

Family: Baetidae   Size: 6-12 mm
Genus: *Callibaetis*
Body Color: Top, gray or brown; bottom, lighter shade of top color
Notice: Females have clear speckled front wings; males' front wings clear with occasional markings
J F M A M J J A S O N D   E, M, W

Within a day after emerging, duns shed their exoskeleton for a final time and become spinners. Interestingly, mayflies are the only insects whose winged adults go through this extra molt. Male spinners gather in large mating swarms from early morning to mid-afternoon. These swarms occur over open water, clear meadows, or in the lee of shoreside vegetation when it is windy. Females fly into these swarms to mate. Fertilized females return to hide in shoreside foliage for about five days, waiting for their eggs to develop. When the eggs are ready to hatch, females fly out to open water and deposit them by dipping their egg-tipped abdomens into the water. The eggs hatch shortly after entering the water. After depositing their eggs, many females end up laying spent on the water. Egg-laying flights generally occur in the calm hours of mornings or evenings and are not synchronized like the mating swarms. Short calm periods on windy days often have the most intense flights as the females race to deposit their eggs.

Gulper Special,
Bunse's *Callibaetis* Spinner, CDC *Callibaetis* Biot Spinner
Hook Size: 12-18

It's difficult to miss mating swarms, but it is very easy to miss spent spinners lying flush on the water. Swarming flights do not mean spinner falls will occur shortly. Females do not return to lay their eggs until five days after they have mated. What you need to watch for are female *Callibaetis* dipping down and touching the water. The numbers of females out laying their eggs varies greatly, from incredibly large masses to a lonely few. Larger numbers are easily seen by both trout and anglers; smaller numbers may well go unnoticed by anglers—but not by the trout. On windy days check sheltered areas. They are often the only areas you will find egg-laying activity and trout feeding on spent spinners. Drifting spent spinners collect in foam lines and along the windward shore. It is difficult to spot feeding fish without spooking them in these areas. Carefully check them from a distance. Trout see these spinners often because of the long duration of the *Callibaetis* hatch, and they become very selective. A good spinner pattern, long leaders, and fine tippets are normally necessary for fishing these spinner falls. Use the cast and wait method to cover any feeding trout. Long casts and low profiles work better than short casts and high profiles. If you have a hard time spotting your flush-floating fly, then try a parachute pattern like the Gulper Special. You can also tie the spinner on as a trailing fly three or four feet behind a more visible dry-fly or indicator. Fine tippets and big fish do not mix well—use with caution.

Gray Drake—Nymph

Family: Siphlonuridae   Size: 12-17 mm
Genus: *Siphlonurus*
Body Color: Tans to grays
Notice: Short antennae, less than 2 1/2 times width of head
J F M A M J J A S O N D

    Siphlonurus nymphs are swimmers. Their tails have interlocking hairs that make them very effective for propelling the nymph forward in five- to ten-inch spurts. Their shorter antennae are the easiest way to tell these mayfly nymphs from other mayfly swimmers found in still waters. *Siphlonurus* mayflies have a one-year life cycle, and with good habitat they often have very dense populations. The nymphs are opportunistic feeders, eating algae, smaller insects, and whatever they can scavenge. Weedy areas in the shallow margins of lakes are their preferred habitat. Mature *Siphlonurus* nymphs migrate from deeper water to exposed plants or to the shore, where they crawl out to emerge and leave their empty nymphal shucks stuck to rocks and plants along the shore. Emergence may occur at any time of the day or night. As long as they stay in the dense foliage of weed beds, these nymphs are safe from prowling trout. But these are restless nymphs, and as they near maturity and start migrating toward shore, they are exposed to trout that often follow them into very shallow water to feed.

Marabou Nymph,
Black Drake, Marabou P.T. Nymph
Hook Size: 6-10

Emergence dates and times vary so much for *Siphlonurus* that the only way to be sure when nymphs are migrating is to check for them. Search for them in the shallows with an insect net or look for their empty nymphal shucks on exposed rocks and plants. Mature nymphs have dark wing pads. These streamlined nymphs are good swimmers. Imitate them with unweighted or lightly weighted, slim, tapered flies. Add any weight toward the front of the hook to give it a jigging action when fished. These flies are often fished close to weeds in shallow water, and nymph patterns that are too heavy will constantly snag weeds and probably spook nearby trout as you work to pull them loose. Use the cast and retrieve method with a floating line and ten- to fifteen-foot leader. These nymphs migrate from deeper water to the shallows, and your fly should follow the same route. Assume a low casting position on the shore and cast your fly out to the deeper water. Allow the fly to sink close to the bottom, and then begin the retrieve. Use steady five- to ten-inch strips, varying the speed from slow to fast. Alternate working the rod tip with short vibrating twitches and not working it at all until the trout show you what retrieve they prefer. Place your fly far enough ahead of any visible feeding fish and allow it to settle. Start the retrieve as the trout nears the fly. Set the hook if you see the trout open its mouth near the fly.

Gray Drake—Spinner

Family: Siphlonuridae   Size: 12-15 mm
Genus: *Siphlonurus*
Body Color: Top, dark grayish brown; bottom, lighter shade of top color
Notice: Large hind wings
J F M A M J J A S O N D

These spinners often have very distinctive markings on the tops of their abdomens. Their clear wings and larger hind wings differentiate them from *Callibaetis* spinners often found in the same waters. Mature *Siphlonurus* nymphs crawl several inches out of the water onto shoreside objects and the duns emerge. Because of this behavior, duns from this family are not normally available to trout and are not a fishable stage. While hidden in shoreside vegetation, duns molt to spinners in two to four days. Spinner flights occur in sheltered areas along the shoreline from mid-morning to late evening, but they generally tend more to the evening hours. Female spinners fly into the swarms and mate. Later, females return to the open water along the lake's margins and, with continued drops to the surface, release all of their eggs until the flies fall spent on the water. At the peak of the hatch, spinner falls can be so dense that spent spinners will seem to cover the water, giving trout many flies from which to choose and causing difficulties for the angler.

Gray Drake Parachute,
Spent Mayfly Gray Drake, Clear Wing Spinner
Hook Size: 8-12

You should try capturing a spinner to help select a fly pattern. Remember that trout see the underside of the fly, so match that color. Use a parachute style fly if you have trouble spotting a flush-floating spinner pattern. As female spinners touch the water laying their eggs, the surface often looks like the start of a rain shower. This is your signal that the spinner fall is beginning. Take a casting position close to the spinner activity and wait for the trout to show. A light spinner fall causes trout to cruise a wide area to feed on spent spinners. They are often wary, so use a long fine leader of nine to fifteen feet. The cast and wait method works best covering these feeding trout. Either cast ahead of a working trout or to an area where a number of trout are working; then let the fly sit, casting again only if the trout move out of the area around the fly. When the spinner fall is very heavy, trout often move along just under the surface and tip their noses up, taking flies in a steady rhythm. This calls for accurate casting. You must place your fly a few feet in front of trout and hope he takes it. If he doesn't, wait until he is at least ten feet away from the fly, and cast again. This kind of fishing can either be great or frustrating, depending on how accurately you cast and how receptive the trout are. Any time you hook a fish under these conditions, pat yourself on the back.

Big Yellow May—Nymph

Family: Ephemeridae   **Size: 18-35 mm**
Genus: *Hexagenia*
Body Color: Pale yellowish-brown
Notice: Tusk-like mandibles
J F M A M J J A S O N D   E M W

With a favorable habitat, *Hexagenia* nymphs reach astounding population densities; as many as 500 nymphs may live within a square foot of lake bottom. In warmer climates, these nymphs mature in one year; in cooler climates, they take two or even three years. They dig U-shaped tunnels into muddy bottoms that are firm enough to keep the burrows from collapsing. Nymphs may live at lake depths of just a few inches or up to fifty feet, but they prefer water from one to ten feet deep. While in their tunnels, nymphs undulate their gills to circulate water. During daylight hours these nymphs do not leave their secure shelters, and trout have little opportunity to feed on them. At night, however, nymphs emerge from their tunnels and feed along the bottom, though the slightest disturbance will send them scurrying back to safety. At maturity nymphs leave their burrows and swim in a strong undulating up-and-down motion to the surface, and the duns quickly emerge from the nymphs. Emergence occurs in the first two or three hours of darkness, but may start earlier on cloudy days. Trout quickly gorge themselves on these emerging nymphs.

Hexagenia Wiggle Nymph, Streamlined Nymph, Strip Nymph
Hook Size: 6-8, 3X Long

An observant angler may notice the worm-like holes of *Hexagenia* nymphs on a muddy bottom. But unless you are present during a hatch, it's difficult to determine if these nocturnally active mayflies live in a lake. It pays to ask a local fly shop if lakes in the area are inhabited by these large mayflies. The nymphs from this family swim with an undulating up-and-down motion, and when at rest, they move their large gills constantly. Fly patterns that mimic these motions are by far the most effective. The nymphs stay close to the bottom unless they are emerging. Use the cast and retrieve method with a sinking line that keeps the fly close to the bottom. On the retrieve work the rod tip with continuous, short, up-and-down movements as you strip in the line, adding pauses to let the fly settle. This is a good technique for searching the water during the evening and night hours throughout the season. Change to a floating fly line and use the sink and retrieve method when mayflies began to emerge. Typically, emerging nymphs swim non-stop from the bottom to the surface. Match this steady ascent with the retrieve, while working the rod tip to impart the nymph's swimming action. Vary the speed of retrieve for both methods. During a hatch, trout quickly gorge themselves on the emerging nymphs as they leave the bottom. Be prepared. Start fishing a nymph an hour before dark or when you see duns flying off the water.

Big Yellow May—Dun

Family: Ephemeridae   Size: 22-35 mm
Genus: *Hexagenia*
Body Color: Top, light tan to bright yellow-olive with distinct
dark markings; bottom, lighter shade of top color, unmarked
J F M A M J J A S O N D   E M W

Hexagenia duns are the easiest of all the mayflies to identify.
They are yellow and big—over two inches long. The nymphs live
in tunnels dug into soft mud bottoms in the margins of a lake. At
maturity nymphs swim to the surface where the duns emerge
quickly from their nymphal shucks and take flight. They are
strong flyers. If it is not windy, they gain elevation quickly and
head for vegetation along the shore. Emergence occurs just before
dark and can last two or three hours. On dark, cloudy days, they
may start emerging a few hours earlier. Lakes with ideal habitat
for these nymphs often have very intense hatches. At the peak
times of this hatch, emerging numbers can be so great that it may
appear that the lake's surface is flying away as all the mayflies lift
off the water. Trout feed heavily on the emerging nymphs at the
start of the hatch. Later in the hatch, if they have not gorged themselves on nymphs, trout feed on the duns. By this time it is often
dark, so the trout's splashy rises are often heard rather than seen.

**Bunse's *Hex* Dun,
Hair Wing Dun, Clark's Big Yellow Mayfly Parachute**
Hook Size: 8-10

Locating the muddy-bottomed emergence areas of lakes where these hatches occur can be difficult. For well-known hatches ask at a local shop, or as evening approaches, watch where locals start to gather on the lake. A large number of discarded nymph shucks floating in the shallows are a sure giveaway that a hatch has occurred. Search for a muddy bottom in the immediate area out from the discovered shucks. Once found, these areas should be fished with nymph patterns before the hatch starts. Remember these spots—they are good year after year (unless the bottom changes), and early in the season, they offer good nymph fishing at dark. Smart fly anglers rig two rods for this hatch—one with a nymph and the other with a dry fly—and fish from a boat or float tube. Position your craft over a muddy-bottomed area, and search the water with a nymph pattern. When trout start working on the surface, switch to the dry fly. Cast toward visible or audible rises. Take up the slack in the fly line, and let the fly sit for five or ten seconds; then lightly twitch it. Repeat this four or five times, and cast again. Fishing in the dark when your fly is not visible requires a hair trigger. Lightly set the hook with short twitch of the rod tip immediately when you hear, see, or feel anything in the area of your fly. The short-twitch hook-set causes little surface disturbance and keeps the fly fishing if it was a false alarm.

Big Yellow May—Spinner

Family: Ephemeridae   **Size: 22-35 mm**
Genus: *Hexagenia*
**Body Color: Female top, light tan to yellow-olive with distinct
dark markings; bottom, lighter shade of top color, unmarked**
J F M A M J J A S O N D E M W

Hexagenia duns entering the terrestrial world must survive
the gauntlet of feeding trout, bats, nighthawks, and other birds.
Those making it to land hide among the foliage. A day or two later,
the duns shed their exoskeleton and transform into sexually
mature spinners. Mating swarms often thirty to sixty feet high
occur over open water and generally start an hour or two after
dark. Copulation takes place in flight and lasts about thirty seconds. After mating, females return to the water; sitting on the surface—generally with their wings in the upright position—each
oviposits 2,000 to 8,000 eggs. This is accomplished by repeatedly
dipping the tip of their abdomens through the surface film and
releasing a large number of eggs each time. After completing their
final reproductive task, the exhausted females collapse spent on
the water and die. Trout feed on both the egg laying and the spent-
wing phases of the spinner falls, but at times they will take one
phase and ignore the other.

Hair Wing Spinner,
Clark's Big Yellow Mayfly Spinner, Bunse's *Hex* Spinner
Hook Size: 8-10

Female spinners start appearing on the water toward the end of the dun emergence. A spinner's body coloration is normally a paler shade of the dun's. Spinners landing on the water with their wings in an upright position look very similar to newly emerged duns. Use a dun or upright-winged pattern during the hatch and into the start of the spinner fall. Their higher silhouettes as they ride on the water are easier to see after dark. As the hatch winds down and the spinner fall increases, there will be more spent mayflies on the water than emerging duns or upright spinners. Trout will start feeding on the dying spinners by keying on the outline of their spent wings on the water. This may be difficult to spot after dark, so change to a spent winged pattern as soon as you feel trout are beginning to ignore the duns. Use the cast and wait method with a floating line. Trout are less spooky after dark so use shorter, stouter leaders, eight or nine feet long, with 3X or 4X tippets. They will turn over larger flies and endure the strikes and fights of the big trout that come after these flies. After completing the cast, take up the slack line and keep your rod tip pointed down toward the water to eliminate any slack between the rod tip and water. This will help you feel a trout taking the fly. Every fifteen or twenty seconds, gently twitch the rod tip to make the fly mimic either the subtle movements of the spinner's abdomen as she wiggles it to free her eggs or the last feeble struggles of a dying mayfly. Twitches also help keep slack out of the line and call a trout's attention to the fly.

Trico—Dun

Family: Leptohyphidae   Size: 3-6 mm
Genus: *Tricorythodes*
**Body Color: Female, olive abdomen and dark brown thorax;
male, dark brown**
Notice: Three long tails and no hind wing
J F M A M J J A S O N D   E, M, W

The nymphs of these small, stout mayflies are crawlers that
live among the weeds or bottom silts in the margin of a lake. These
nymphs spend most of their time hidden from trout. This concealment, along with their small size, makes their nymphal stage the
least important to anglers. The nymphs grow rapidly, and there
are often two generations a year, one emerging in June and July
and another emerging from August through October. Emergence
takes place in the shallow margins of the lake. Duns emerge from
mature nymphs that either crawl out on above-water objects or
float to the surface. Male *Tricorythodes* duns generally emerge at
night or early morning, followed by the female duns that begin
emerging in the early morning and often continue until late morning. Female duns are typically larger than males and have olive-
colored bodies instead of the males' dark brown. Lakes with suitable habitat produce incredible numbers of these mayflies, pro-
viding fishable hatches daily throughout each generation's emergence period. The first-generation hatches often overlap into the
start of second-generation emergence. Trout cruise the lake margins in anticipation of these emerging mayflies.

CDC Trico Emerger,
Gulper Special, Little Olive Parachute
Hook Size: 18-24

Trico nymphs are crawlers, easily collected with a small aquarium net passed through the silt and weeds in the shallows. If you find a large number of these small robust nymphs with dark wing pads (indicating they are mature), be prepared for their morning emergence. The sizes and colors of these mayflies vary, so collect a dun early in the hatch and match your fly to it. At the start of a hatch trout often cruise at random, feeding on emerging duns. These trout are often very cautious and difficult to deceive. The calm morning waters allow them ample time to inspect each fly before taking or refusing it. The CDC Trico Emerger is a good pattern for these picky trout. As the hatch progresses and the number of duns on the water increases, trout lose some of their caution and start rising at regular intervals, often in well-defined straight or oval routes. Use the cast and wait method with a floating line and a leader of fifteen feet or longer with 6X or 7X tippet. Cast the fly ten to fifteen feet in front of cruising trout to avoid spooking them. Fly placement is critical; if it lands more than a foot from the trout's route, it is often ignored. If the fly is ignored, wait for the trout to leave the vicinity of the fly before recasting to avoid spooking it. It is common to see pods of feeding trout traveling together for this hatch. Place your fly on the outer edge of the pods to avoid lining them. An hour or more into the hatch, Trico spinners start to appear on the water. Continue using a dun pattern as long as trout are interested in it.

Trico—Spinner

Family: Leptohyphidae   Size: 3-6 mm
Genus: Tricorythodes
**Body Color: Female, grayish abdomen and black thorax; male,
black abdomen and thorax**
J F M A M J J A S O N D   E, M, W

Generally male Trico duns emerge at night and females in the early morning. They fly to shoreside foliage, and the transformation from dun to spinner takes from a few minutes to a couple of hours. Mating flights occur in the calm morning hours shortly after the duns begin emerging. Females fly into the swarms and mate, then return to the shoreside foliage to pump their fertilized eggs out to the ends of their abdomens. This takes about thirty minutes. The egg-laden females return immediately to the water and deposit their eggs, then die spent on the water. After mating, the exhausted male spinners fall to the surface and are often the first spinners to show on the water, with the females arriving about half-an-hour later. During the last part of the hatch, it is common to have duns and spinners on the water at the same time. If the hatch is light, trout may key on one form and ignore the other. Mating flights will not occur if there is a steady wind blowing, but any calm period on a windy morning will start the mating flights. At the peak of the hatch cycle, spent Trico spinners can literally cover the water. Trout often cruise just below the surface and, with a steady rhythm, raise their heads to noisily gulp down large numbers of spinners.

Trico Parachute,
Krystal Flash Spinner, Trico Poly Spinner
Hook Size: 18-24

When most anglers talk about fishing the Trico hatch, they are usually referring to the spinner falls that occur at the same time daily for the duration of the hatch. When great numbers of spinners fall on the calm, still waters of the morning, they draw most of the lake's larger trout to feed. For anglers it can be a time of great pleasure or frustration depending on their preparedness, casting skills, patience, and luck. You must match your fly to the natural. These small fly patterns and wary fish require fine leaders between fifteen to twenty feet long, tapered to a 6X or 7X tippet. Soft-tip rods are necessary with these light tippets to reduce the chance of breaking off fish on the strike. Use the cast and wait method to imitate the motionless spinner. For any chance of a hook-up, the fly must placed five to ten feet ahead, and directly in the path, of feeding trout. During heavy spinner falls when the water is covered with spinners, trout often follow a set route and will not deviate from it as they feed in steady, gulping rises. When fewer flies are on the water at the start of a hatch or during lighter spinner falls, trout are not as set in their habits but are often more cautious. Rather than trying to cover all the rising trout, be patient and stalk a single trout. This will enable you to learn the trout's feeding rhythm and route. Then if you have a little luck to accompany a well-placed fly on a light tippet, the trout will not hesitate taking it.

Chapter 5

True Flies

Midge is a name given to flies in the family Chironomidae from the order Diptera, which means two winged (di = two and ptera = wing). The Chironomidae family in North America contains more than 175 genera and 1,000 species. All midges have similar body shapes—just size and color vary—so it is not necessary to identify them beyond the family level. The name "midge" reflects the small size of most of the species, but not all. They undergo complete metamorphosis—egg, larva, pupa, and adult. Trout feed on the last three of these stages.

Damselflies and dragonflies are classified in the order Odonata. "Odon" is from the Greek meaning "tooth" and refers to the sharp teeth on their extendible, hinged lower jaws, which aid these predators in capturing their prey. This order is divided into two suborders: Anisoptera for dragonflies and Zygoptera for damselflies. Odonata have an incomplete metamorphosis; there is no pupa stage—just egg, nymph, and adult. Trout feed on both damselfly nymphs and adults, but only on the nymph of the dragonfly since the adult insect is such a strong flier that it's seldom available to trout.

Water boatmen, in the family Corixidae, and back swimmers, in the family Notonectidae, are from the order Hemiptera. They have incomplete metamorphosis. Trout feed on both families when available. The smaller water boatmen—covered later in the text—are more common and abundant than back swimmers. But, the shapes, habits, and habitats of both families are similar, and the same fishing techniques can be used after choosing a fly to match the size and color of the natural.

Water beetles are in the order Coleoptera, which includes both aquatic and terrestrial beetles. There are large numbers of aquatic beetles, but only two are of interest to stillwater anglers. One of these beetles is covered in this chapter, but the techniques and patterns described can be used for the other beetles as well. Water beetles undergo complete metamorphosis, but only the larvae and adults are available to trout.

Alderflies, from the order Megaloptera, also go through complete metamorphosis. The larvae and pupae are seldom available to trout, and are not covered in this text. These flies were named for the alder trees, where the adults congregate, that line the shores of rivers and lakes in England.

Midge—Larva

Order: Diptera   Size: 2-20 mm
Family: Chironomidae
Body Colors: Black, browns, creams, greens, or reds
J F M A M J J A S O N D   E, M, W

Midge larvae have worm-like bodies with a well-developed head and two pairs of prolegs—fleshy, leg-like appendages—one pair on the first segment of the thorax and the other on the last segment of the abdomen. Even with the aid of these legs they are not very mobile. A few red midge larvae, known as "bloodworms," get their color from a hemoglobin-like substance in their bodies that allows them to extract more oxygen from the water and thus enables them to live in habitats with low oxygen levels. The length of their life cycles vary. Midges living in warmer waters may go through several generations a year; those in cooler waters or areas with shorter warm seasons—such as high-elevation lakes—normally have one generation a year. Midge larvae are bottom-dwellers that occupy most areas of a lake. They often live in tubes or cases, though some species are free-living. Most midge larvae feed on organic materials, but a few species are predaceous. When food is sparse the larvae roam for it, generally near or after sunset. The tremendous numbers of larvae in a lake provide a reliable food source for trout most of the year, but when midge pupae are available trout often ignore the larvae and concentrate on the pupae.

Brassie,
Krystal Flash Midge, Swannundaze Midge
Hook Size: 10-16

The often dense populations of midge larvae in lakes make them an important food source for trout throughout the year, especially in higher-elevation lakes. In most lakes, when other insects are scarce in spring and fall, midge larvae supply a good part of a trout's diet. Because the larvae are not easily collected, it is difficult to verify their color and size. Bloodworms are often predaceous and tend to roam; thus red or maroon-colored midge patterns are a good starting point, followed by greens and browns. You can also tie on two or three flies of different colors as droppers or trailing flies and let the trout choose. Most midge larvae in lakes are larger than the stream-living members of their family, so try using hook sizes 12-16 when you are unable to verify the natural's size. Use the cast and retrieve method with a sinking or sink-tip line. Midge larvae spend their lives on the bottom, and that's where you should fish your flies, retrieving them slowly with added pauses to imitate the natural's movement. Remember to keep your rod tip down close to the water to eliminate any line slack. This will help you detect the gentle takes of trout. Heavy wave action often sweeps larvae off the bottom into the upper water levels. The period after a storm is a good time to imitate these drifting larvae with the wind-drift method and a sink-tip or floating line. Fish the edges of drop-offs along shorelines and shoals where the midges tend to collect and trout feed on them.

Midge—Pupa

Order: Diptera   Size: 2-20 mm
Family: Chironomidae
Body Colors: Black, browns, creams, greens, or reds
J F M A M J J A S O N D   E, M, W

Pupation occurs after midge larvae go through a final molt and attain their maximum size. Within their tubes or under bottom silt, mature larvae spin cocoons and seal themselves inside. The encased pupae develop quickly, often reaching maturity within a week. Once the transformation is complete, the pupae leave the safety of their cocoons and swim by wiggling their abdomens with their heads pointed toward the surface. They travel slowly, straight up from the bottom, with frequent pauses. Once they reach the surface, they must break through the surface film. On windy days, escaping through the lighter surface film tension is easier and emergence occurs quickly, but on calm warm days, which produce a heavier surface film tension, the vertically-suspended pupae require a longer time to break through. Emergence tends to be heaviest in the spring, but occurs in all the ice-free months of the year. Pupae can emerge anywhere from the shallow lake margins to mid-lake water less than fifty feet deep. Trout feed heavily on the pupae both when the insects leave the bottom and when they hang in the surface film.

Seed Bead Midge Pupa, Suspender Midge, TDC

Hook Size: 12-18

Midges can emerge anywhere on the lake, so watch for surface activity or feeding birds. Finding pupae suspended in the film or capturing an adult will allow you to match size and color with your pupa imitation. If none are found, use the trailing or dropper system to fish a couple of different colors and sizes of pupae imitations until you find the one trout are taking. To imitate pupae leaving the bottom and swimming to the surface, use the sink and retrieve method with a floating line and a leader long enough to reach the bottom. Retrieve the fly slowly, adding short pauses every foot. Watch where the line enters the water and set the hook at the slightest pause or twitch. A strike indicator will aid in detecting takes and setting your fishing depth. Remember, midge pupae are slow swimmers, and they rise vertically through the water. When fishing deeper water, use a sinking line and cast out just enough line to reach the bottom below you. Then after the line has sunk and is hanging straight down, fish the fly straight up. When trout are feeding on pupae in the surface film, use a floating line with the cast and wait method. To keep the fly close to the surface, either put floatant on your leader within a foot of the fly or use a fly with a foam head to keep it hanging vertically like the natural. For all the above methods, it is important to anchor your craft both in the front and back to keep it from swinging and dragging your fly. Fishing a pupa imitation properly may seem slow, but it will consistently take trout.

Midge—Adult

Order: Diptera   Size: 2-20 mm
Family: Chironomidae
Body Colors: Black, browns, creams, greens, or reds
J F M A M J J A S O N D   E, M, W

After the midge pupa has worked its way through the surface film, the back of its pupal shuck splits open and the adult emerges and flies off. On cooler days adults may sit on the water for a time, but on warm days they leave the water shortly after emerging. The adults fly to shoreside vegetation where the females wait for their eggs to develop and the males for mating swarms to begin. These non-biting insects are often confused with adult mosquitoes, which rest with their hind legs in the air. Male midges, identified by their plume-like antennae, form mating flights during calm periods of the day or night. Females fly into the swarm where mating takes place. These swarms may be so dense that the buzzing noise produced by them can sound like the loud buzz of a high-voltage power line. After mating, females return to the water and lay their eggs. Some fly over the water and repeatedly drop to the surface, dipping their abdomens through the surface film to release a number of eggs. Others fly to exposed objects and crawl below the surface to lay their eggs. Whenever a large number of midge adults become available, trout feed on them.

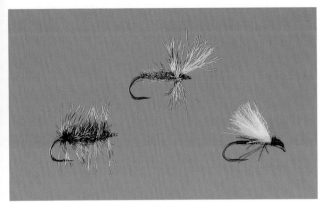

Parachute Midge Emerger, Griffith's Gnat, CDC Midge Adult
Hook Size: 14-20

Midge adults are not as easily captured by trout as are the larvae and pupae, but under the right conditions trout feed on them.
On warm, calm days during a hatch, most of the trout concentrate
on pupae suspended beneath the surface, ignoring the adults that
spend little time on the water. When trout are working close to the
surface, use an emerger pattern that you can see, or hang a pupa
imitation below a dry-fly adult pattern. Place your cast ahead of or
near the feeding trout. The cast and wait method with a slight
twitch of the fly added every fifteen or twenty seconds imitates
the natural and attracts the trout's attention. On cold days, adults
spend more time on the water, and trout have greater opportunity
to feed on them. Egg-laying females also offer trout a chance to
feed. During windy condition, adults are often blown into the
water and trapped there. Feeding trout cruise the foam lines and
windward shorelines where stillborn, crippled, or spent adults
collect. All of these conditions bring trout up to feed on the surface. To imitate these emerging or trapped insects, use the cast and
wait method and place your fly ahead of feeding trout. Let the fly
sit without movement; if the trout does not take the fly, wait until
it has passed by, and give it a little twitch to attract its attention.

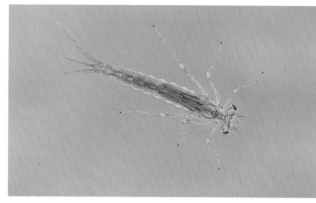

Damselfly—Nymph

Order: Odonata   Size: 15-30 mm
Suborder: Zygoptera
Family: Coenagrionidae
Body Colors: Browns to greens
Notice: Three leaf-like gills at the end of a slender body
J F M A M J J A S O N D   E, M, W

Damselflies normally go through a one-year life cycle, although two generations a year is not uncommon in warm climates. Large numbers of mature nymphs typically occur early in the season, with numbers decreasing as they hatch. Nymphs spend most of their time in and around submerged vegetation, which provides them with prey and shelter from predators. Chameleon-like, their body-color changes to match its surroundings. Nymphs normally wait in ambush for their prey, and move slowly when necessary. Aided by their paddle-like gills, they swim with slow side-to-side, minnow-like movements for a foot or so, then pause to rest. At maturity, nymphs leave their protective cover and begin swimming toward shore or any object projecting above the water, and then crawl out on a dry surface to emerge. This migration generally occurs en masse, mid-to-late morning, with the nymphs swimming close to the surface. It is during this emergence migration that damselfly nymphs are easy prey for trout, which eagerly take them with quick rolls and slashes.

Henry's Damselfly Nymph, Warren's Damsel, Brown Eyed Damsel

Hook Size: 8-14

Because of their normal one-year life cycle and their habit of hiding in the weeds, damselfly nymphs tend to attract more attention from trout when they start emerging than they do earlier in the season. But smaller nymph patterns can still produce trout in the early part of the season and in the fall. The fly must be fished in or close to submerged vegetation using a sinking or sink-tip line to keep the fly close to the bottom. Use the cast and retrieve method with a slow retrieve to imitate the slow crawl of the natural. Empty nymphal shucks stuck on objects along the shore advertise that a hatch is in progress. During the nymphs' swimming migration toward shore in mid-to-late morning, trout cruise the shallow margins of the lake feeding on them. These nymphs swim close to the surface, so use an unweighted or lightly weighted fly and a floating line to keep the fly close to the surface. Use the cast and retrieve method, and place the fly ahead of the trout. Imitate the naturals' swimming action by retrieving the fly with slow, one-foot strips of line while adding a four-inch side-to-side vibration to the tip of your lowered rod. Pause briefly after each one-foot strip. In shallow water trout are spooky, so a low profile and casting low over the water will increase your chances for hook-ups. Trout follow these nymphs right to the water's edge, so stalking the shoreline of a lake during this hatch can produce some fantastic fishing.

Damselfly—Adult

Order: Odonata   Size: 25-40 mm
Suborder: Zygoptera
Family: Coenagrionidae
Body Colors: Blue, brown, green, red, yellow
Notice: Long slender body; wings rest along the top of the abdomen
J F M A M J J A S O N D   E, M, W

Shortly after the nymphs crawl out of the water the adults
emerge from the nymphal shucks. When the newly-hatched tan-
colored adults are able to fly, they head for the protection of shoreside vegetation. At this time they are weak fliers and during
windy conditions many of them end up on the water. After these
recently emerged adults reach safety, it takes a few hours for their
bodies to harden and take on their final adult colors. Adults have
an average life span of four to six weeks. To survive, they must
feed, which they do by capturing smaller insects while in flight.
With few exceptions, damsels fly only when it is sunny and usually only in the afternoon; they stop flying if a cloud blocks the sun.
Mating takes place in the air or on objects near the water. The male
grasps the female behind the head and they fly off together to
deposit the eggs, or the female will fly out to exposed vegetation
and crawl underwater to deposit her eggs. Sudden or gusty winds
often knock these flying adults into the water where trout eagerly
feed on them.

Braided Butt Damsel,
Parachute Damsel, Shewey's Adult Damsel
Hook Size: 10-12, 3X Long

Although damselfly adults may not be as important to anglers as the nymphs, anglers that spend any time on lakes with good damselfly populations will regret not having a few adult fly patterns in their box. Gusty winds cause many newly-hatched, feeding, or egg-laying adults to end up in the water. Since adults generally fly only when the sun is shining, the time for fishing these patterns is during bright sunny days when you see good numbers of adults in the air. Check foam lines and other areas where adults trapped in the surface film collect during windy conditions. Place your fly at least ten feet in front of any visible cruising trout and let it sit. If the trout heads in another direction, twitch the fly once to see if you can draw his attention back to it before you cast again. Trout take these flies with very deliberate rises, so don't set the hook too soon. When you notice females landing on exposed aquatic vegetation and crawling underwater to lay their eggs, cast your fly to the edges of exposed weeds and pull the dry fly under water. Then use a slow retrieve to imitate the submerged adults. If more depth is needed, use a sink-tip line, but remember, females lay their eggs close to the surface, so don't fish too deep. When trout jump out of the water after low-flying adults, immediately place your fly on the water where the fish rose. Using damselfly adult patterns offers you a chance to catch large trout during a time of the day that most anglers write off as unproductive.

Dragonfly—Nymph—Climber

Order: Odonata   Size: 30-50 mm
Suborder: Anisoptera
Family: Aeshnidae
Body Colors: Brown, grays, and greens
Notice: Long, hourglass-shaped body
J F M **A M J J A S O N**   **E, M, W**

Dragonflies have a two- to three-year life cycle with the adults living for an average of four to six weeks after emerging. The large nymphs are very aggressive predators and well deserve their name. But it was probably the colorful, strong flying, predatory, and very territorial adults that resulted in these insects being called "dragonflies." The adults of this family generally have large, dark bodies with blue or green markings, and when at rest, they hold their clear wings outspread. They seldom end up on the water and offer no fishable hatch for anglers. But the presence of adults flying is a good indication that nymphs are migrating toward shore to emerge, and they are of importance to anglers. These nymphs climb around aquatic vegetation actively pursuing prey, which they catch by shooting out their extendible hinged lower lip with a speed too quick for your eyes to follow. When disturbed they use water forced though their rectum—where their gills are located—to jet away in short two- to three-inch bursts. Dragonfly nymphs do not migrate en masse toward shore as do damselflies. But they are such large meals that it doesn't take many nymphs moving toward shore to interest trout.

Rabbit Strip Dragon,
Bottom Walker, All Rounder Dragonfly Nymph
Hook Size: 4-8, 3X Long

Because of their two- to three-year life cycle, these nymphs are available to trout most of the season. But since they spend most of their time pursuing prey in heavy weed cover, they are not easy for trout to catch. When they leave the protective cover and start migrating toward shore to emerge, they are most vulnerable to feeding trout. Adults of these nymphs generally have blue or green bodies with clear wings, and when you observe them around a lake you will know that a pattern imitating a climber dragonfly nymph will catch a trout's attention. The weight of the fly and type of fly line used depends on the depth of water and degrees of weed cover to be fished. In shallow weedy areas use a floating line with an unweighted or lightly weighted fly. The Bottom Walker's moose mane hackle acts as a weed guard, making it an effective imitation to use in weedy areas. In deeper water around weedy areas use a sinking or sink-tip line with an unweighted or lightly weighted fly so that the fly sinks slowly and floats above the sinking fly line. This will position the fly just above or in the top layer of weeds and reduce hang-ups. Use the cast and retrieve method with a countdown to find the proper depth to fish. Alternate the retrieve to imitate the nymphs slow crawling pace and their two- to four-inch bursts of speed.. Think of a nymph crawling along the bottom that is startled and jets off for a few feet before it pauses to rest. Trout cannot resist these nymphs, and the takes are often furious.

Dragonfly—Nymph—Sprawler

Order: Odonata   Size: 20-30 mm
Suborder: Anisoptera
Family: Libellulidae
Body Colors: Browns and greens—colors of substrate
Notice: Oval squat body, often covered with fine hairs
J F M A M J J A S O N   E, M, W

These dragonflies have a two- to three-year life cycle. At maturity the nymphs crawl out of the water to emerge. The beautiful adults with black-patterned wings and brilliant red or blue bodies live an average of four to six weeks after emerging. They are strong fliers and seldom end up on the water. The body color of the nymph normally matches that of the substrate and is often camouflaged by silt and debris collected in its body hairs. Sprawlers do not actively pursue prey like the climber dragonfly nymphs that are also common in lakes. Instead they sprawl on bottoms with abundant wood or plant debris and wait in ambush for prey to approach closely enough to be grabbed with their extendible lower lip. When alarmed, they can compress their abdomens to shoot water out their rectums and jet away in two- to four-inch bursts. Unless they are disturbed or caught moving, hiding nymphs do not offer trout many opportunities for a meal.

Henry's Dragon Nymph, Gierach Dragon, Janssen Dragon
Hook Size: 6-10, 2X Long

These sprawler dragonfly nymphs spend most of their time hiding in ambush on bottom with wood and plant debris. They do not actively pursue prey as nymphs in the climber family, nor do they migrate en masse to emerge. But it does not take many of these large nymphs to keep the trout interested. Identifying the bright-bodied and black-marked winged adults from this family will help you choose a nymph pattern of the right shape. These are short, squat nymphs, so your pattern should imitate that profile, with a color to match the lake bottom. The Gierach Dragon pattern, with its heavy beard, is almost weedless, making it ideal for fishing around weedy areas. Depending on the water depth, use a floating, sink-tip, or sinking line. Fish the fly close to the bottom using the cast and retrieve method with a countdown. The retrieve should imitate the slow crawl of the nymph. Every couple of feet during the retrieve, give a few quick four-inch strips to jump the fly off the bottom and get it moving like a startled nymph. Then pause to let it settle before starting the slow retrieve again. Trout often hit this nymph pattern hard during the retrieve. But if they pick it up as the fly settles during the pause there may be little indication of the take, so watch for any movement of the line where it enters the water.

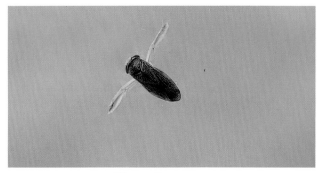

Water Boatmen

Order: Hemiptera   **Size: 6-12 mm**
Family: Corixidae
**Body Colors: Backs—browns, tans and greens; belly—lighter
shade of back color**
J F M A M J J A S O N D   E, M, W

Water boatmen were named for their means of moving in the water. The rear pair of hairy legs are used like a set of oars on a small boat, mimicking the same pulsing forward motion. They develop from egg to nymph to adult in a one-year cycle, but the nymph and adult look alike and behave similarly. The nymph lacks the adult's wings, which develop in the last of the five instars. The adults do not emerge or hatch like mayflies or caddisflies; they continue living underwater and do not take flight until they are ready to mate. Adults typically reach maturity in the fall, over-winter, then mate and lay their eggs in the spring. Both adults and nymphs have no gills, so they collect air from the surface, trapping a bubble against their bodies to use as an air supply while underwater. Because of this reliance on surface air, they are restricted to shallow waters. They live and feed in and around weedy areas. Weedy, alkaline lakes often produce immense numbers of water boatmen, which can be a major food source for resident trout. But in most lakes the adults are important to trout and anglers primarily from the fall through the early spring when there are fewer hatches and less insect activity.

Corixid,
Boatman, Sparkle Boatman
Hook Size: 12-18

Normally, water boatmen are an important food source for trout in winter and early spring when the adult insects attain their largest size. They do not often leave the protection of the weeds and are seldom found in open water unless there is a weedy shoal in the area. Because of their need for surface air, they live in water less than five feet deep. The lighter colored underside and darker upper-body colors often match that of the substrate. To mimic the air bubble that the naturals carry, imitations should have some sparkle to them. In water under three feet deep, use a floating line with a lightly weighted fly and the cast and retrieve method. The naturals move in one- to three-inch spurts, so on the retrieve use a moderate strip and add a slight vibrating twitch to your rod tip to mimic the natural's jerky swimming style. When cruising fish are present, place the fly far enough ahead of them so that it has time to settle to the fish's depth. Wait until the trout are close to the fly before starting the retrieve. In deeper water, use the sink and retrieve method to imitate a water boatmen's return to the surface to replenish its air supply. Fish cruise the outer edges of shallow weedy areas feeding on careless nymphs. Trout generally feel secure enough to venture into the shallows to feed on water boatmen when there is a chop on the water or during low light conditions. It's hard to spot trout under these conditions. Watch for any surface disturbance that gives away a trout's position; quickly place the fly within a foot of it and begin the retrieve.

Predacious Diving Beetle—Larva

Order: Coleoptera   Size: 2-70 mm
Family: Dytiscidae
Body Color: Brown, tan, or olive
Notice: Large sickle-shaped mandibles
J F M A M J J A S O N D   E, M, W

In the spring, adult water beetles lay their eggs, which hatch
in one to three weeks. These newly-hatched larvae are fast growing, normally reaching maturity by late summer. They then crawl
out of the water to pupate. The larvae are fierce predators, com-
monly called water tigers, that try to catch anything smaller than
themselves. Their large hollow mandibles are used to capture prey
and to inject enzymes into it. The enzymes break down the vic-
tim's tissues, which allow it to be sucked out through the
mandibles. Handle water beetle larvae with care as they can inflict
a painful bite. Most species breath air from the surface, taking it in
through tubes located at the tips of their abdomens, and are thus
restricted to living in shallow water. The larvae are feeble swimmers and must use vegetation as their roadway to the surface for
air or for stalking prey. The often dense aquatic habitats where
these beetles live make them marginal trout food. But there are
many lakes that have very dense populations of water beetles,
which can make them an important food source. Such lakes often
have large, shallow, weedy areas—prime habitat for these larvae.

Creeper,
Simulator, Woolly Worm
Hook Size: 6-12, 3X Long

Even though many anglers do not fish water beetle imitations or consider the larvae an important food source for trout, they have probably caught trout on flies that were taken for these larvae. If you spend any time on lakes you are going to run into trout feeding on these larvae, most often in shallow weedy areas. Fish move into these fertile regions to feed on insects and crustaceans, and whenever water beetle larvae are available trout will take them. Because of their one-year life cycle, these large larvae are only available in the summer months. When you find large numbers of them in the shallows of the lake, it makes good sense to fish a fly that imitates them. The naturals spend most of their time on weeds close to the surface for easy access to their air supply. Larvae wait for prey to come within striking distance then lunge out and grab it. A weedless, lightly weighted pattern such as the creeper is ideal for fishing this insect's weedy habitat. If you tie flies, it is easy to put a looped nylon weed guard on flies fished in weedy areas. Cast to openings and edges of weed beds using a floating line with the cast and retrieve method. Vary the retrieve with slow strips, pauses, and sudden short jumps to imitate the movements of the natural. Fishing weedy areas necessitates the use of stronger leaders and requires that the rod tip be raised quickly after hooking a trout to keep from snagging the line and breaking off the fish.

Predacious Diving Beetle—Adult

Order: Coleoptera   Size: 3-25 mm
Family: Dytiscidae
Body Color: Black or brown
Notice: Hairy hind legs
J F M A M J J A S O N D   E, M, W

In the late summer months when beetle larvae are mature, they crawl from the water and find a hiding spot to pupate. After two to four weeks, adults emerge from their pupal shucks and return to the water and once again lead an aquatic life. They overwinter by either hibernating or staying active. In the spring they mate, lay their eggs, and die. Aided by hairy rear legs that act as oars, the adults are good swimmers. As with the larvae, adults must go to the surface to collect air, which they carry trapped under their hard front wings. This limits the depth of water in which they can live to four or five feet. Some adults are able to get air from bubbles that collect on underwater plants. The adults, like the larvae, are predators, but instead of the larva's sickle-like mandibles, the adults have chewing mouth parts. They also differ from the larvae in their method of capturing prey. Where the larvae often wait in ambush, the adults crawl or rapidly swim though the weeds in search of prey. This hunting activity and the constant trips to the surface to replenish their air supplies make the adults vulnerable to trout.

Swimming Beetle,
Soft Hackle, Deep Sparkle Pupa
Hook Size: 4-12, 2X Long

In the spring and fall, when there are few other hatches, adult beetles are active in the shallow weedy margins of lakes. They often live in very dense vegetation where trout have little chance of feeding on them. But in lakes with a large population, beetles are available often enough that trout take their imitations well into the summer months, long after the mating adult beetles have disappeared. Trout take these speedy swimmers violently, often leaving large boils on the surface. To imitate hunting adults in water deeper than three feet, use a sink-tip fly line to keep the fly down during the retrieve. Use the countdown and cast and retrieve methods to get the fly close to submerged weeds. The retrieve should imitate the natural's quick, jerky swimming movements. As you strip in the line, vibrate the rod tip and add pauses every three or four feet. In water shallower than three feet, use a floating line with the cast and retrieve method. Start retrieving the line and vibrating the rod tip soon after the fly hits the water. If the water is deep enough, add pauses and let the fly settle; then lift the rod to mimic an adult rising to the surface for air. Adult water beetle patterns are good for searching large areas of weed beds in the morning and evening or to cast ahead of visible cruising trout, beginning the retrieve as they near the fly.

Alderfly—Adult

Order: Megaloptera   Size: 10-15 mm
Family: Sialidae
Body Color: Black or drake brown
Notice: Hairless, tent-like wings
J F M A M J J A S O N D   E, M, W

Alderfly larvae live among the debris that collects on the bottom of shallow margins in lakes and ponds. They are voracious predators, but seldom leave cover in the pursuit of prey. When the larvae reach maturity in the spring or early summer, they leave the water to pupate in burrows along the shore. Pupation lasts two or three weeks. The adults emerge and gather on the shoreside vegetation. They are weak, clumsy fliers and when disturbed they normally prefer to run rather than fly. The adults mate among the shoreside vegetation, and later the females deposit their eggs on foliage that hangs out over the water. The eggs hatch in a week or two and the larvae drop into the water. Alderflies have a one-year life cycle. The only time that alderflies are available to trout in any numbers is in the adult stage as they congregate on foliage hanging over the water. Windy conditions account for most of the adults found in the water. Few adults escape the water once there, and they begin to sink as soon as they start struggling. Where heavy hatches occur, trout cruise tree-lined shores hunting for these struggling or drowned flies.

Deer Hair Caddis, Alder, Morse's Alder Fly
Hook Size: 8-12

Lakes with good populations of alderflies generally have margins with dense, debris-filled bottoms and shoreline foliage hanging over the water. Adults emerge from spring to mid-summer. The appearance of adults on shoreside foliage signals the time to fish an alderfly imitation. These poor fliers become active as the day warms, and this warming normally brings afternoon winds that shake the shoreside foliage and sweep the insects out over the water. Many of these scattered adults hit the surface, and once in the water they struggle on top for a short time before sinking, where they continue to struggle until they die. This scenario occurs often enough that trout will cruise brushy shorelines in search of alderfly adults. Trout take adults struggling on the surface whenever large numbers are on the water, but it is the sunken adults, struggling or dead, that seem to draw the most attention from trout. Use a floating fly line with a nine- to twelve-foot leader. When using a dry fly, cast toward working fish and let it sit a few moments before adding a few slight twitches. With wet flies, use a retrieve with short, slow, strips and added pauses that mimic the natural's movements. Wherever alderflies are found, fish along those shores, concentrating on areas that offer trout cover—logs, boulders, weed beds, and deep water.

Chapter 6

Crustaceans, Leeches, Forage Fish, Terrestrials

Some crustaceans, from the phylum Arthropoda, class Crustacea, are important to fly anglers—they are the scuds in the order Amphipoda, and crayfish in the order Decapoda. Lakes blessed with dense populations of scuds typically produce very large trout. Crayfish do not supply the steady staple food source that scuds offer trout, but when available, fleeing crayfish are seldom passed up by trout.

Leeches are from the phylum Annelida, class Hirudinea. They are found in most lakes and rivers, often in very large numbers. They are also known as blood suckers. Some were, and are, being used by physicians for bloodletting, but only a small number of the 63 freshwater species fall in this group. Many people have an aversion to them, but trout do not.

Forage fish include a large group of smaller fish that are eaten by trout. It is beyond the scope of this book to cover all of them. Most of these fish can be placed into three groups: bottom dwellers, shallow-water dwellers, and open-water schooling dwellers. Each group looks and behaves differently. To be successful in most lakes, fly anglers need only carry a few flies of different sizes from each group and understand how the fish in each group act.

Terrestrial insects become trapped in the water often enough that trout selectively feed on them, and any angler caught without a closely matching pattern often goes fishless. Flying ants (order: Hymenoptera), beetles (order: Coleoptera), and grasshoppers (order: Orthoptera) are the terrestrials that most often end up in the water. Finding them on the water is not something you can count on, but there are exceptions. Ants tend to mate at certain times of the year, and when the mating flights occur over open water, both trout and anglers eagerly await their arrival. Wind is why most terrestrials end up on the water and for concentrating them in certain areas where trout feed on them.

Scuds

Order: Amphipoda   **Size: 3-25 mm**
Body Color: Olive, tan, or gray
J F M A M J J A S O N D

North America has three families of scuds and two are important to fly anglers. Scuds, in the family Gammaridae, are the
largest, ranging from 10 to 25 mm. Of the eight genera in this family, *Gammarus* are the most important. They occur in fertile lakes
with high levels of calcium, which is necessary for the development of their exoskeletons. Scuds of the genus *Hyalella* in the family Talitridae are small, 3-5 mm, and have a greater chemical and
temperature tolerance. They occur over a wider range and are
often found in less-productive or higher-elevation lakes. Both families often occupy the same waters, and other than the size difference, their appearance and behavior is similar. Scuds live in the
shallow margins of lakes. Weed beds are their preferred habitat,
but they are also found in bottom debris and rocky areas. They
feed on living or decomposing plant and animal matter. When the
water temperature reaches the mid-sixties, the males and females
couple and mate. They have multiple broods throughout the summer. The orange-colored eggs and newly-hatched young are carried on the underside of the female in brood sacs until they are
shed. Scuds are light-sensitive, feeding at night or in low light
conditions and hiding during the day. Typically they swim one to
six inches before pausing to rest. Where scuds occur, trout grow
large feeding on them.

Scud,
Gammarus-Hyalella Scud, Ostrich Scud
Hook Size: 6-18

Trout will feed on scuds all year if these crustaceans are available, only slowing their feeding when other insects are hatching. Natural lakes tend to have denser populations than reservoirs with fluctuating water levels. When good populations of scuds are present in lakes, they are often found clinging to aquatic weeds picked from the shallows. It is important to match the size and color of the naturals. Scuds lifted from the water curl their bodies into a ball, but when moving or swimming in the water their bodies are stretched almost straight, so use a straight-bodied pattern. Orange-colored patterns may be used to imitate egg-carrying females during the summer, but body colors normally match that of the substrate. If you are not sure what color pattern to use, start with one that matches the color of the bottom. Scuds spend most of their time close to the bottom, slowly crawling or swimming at slow to moderate speeds for two to six inches, then pausing to rest for a few seconds. Use the cast and retrieve method; keep the fly close to the bottom, and vary the retrieve to match the natural's erratic movements. In shallow water, use a floating line with a lightly weighted fly; in water deeper than three feet, use a slow-sinking or sink-tip line with an unweighted or lightly weighted fly. Scuds are sensitive to light. Fish their imitations during early mornings, evenings, and overcast days.

Crayfish

Order: Decapoda   Size: 1-130 cm
Family: Astacidae
Body Color: Shades of browns, olives to orange
J F M A M J J A S O M N D   E, M, W

Crayfish have an average life span of two years, but may live as long as seven years. They may grow to a length of five inches, but average about four. Two front claws used for protection and feeding are larger on the males, which often raise them in a defensive posture. Four pairs of legs enable crayfish to crawl in all directions. If lost, these limbs can be regenerated. When disturbed they swim in reverse using quick underbody thrusts from their large jointed tails to propel them in foot-long bursts away from danger. To streamline their bodies and reduce drag when swimming, they tuck their legs forward and hold their claws straight in front of them; all these appendages trail behind them as they skitter away in reverse. They feed on living or dead plants and animals, which are caught and held with their claws. Most of their daylight hours are spent hiding in dark recesses under rocks, logs, and weeds, or in holes they dig in the bottom. They are more active at night or during low light conditions when they crawl from their shelters to hunt food. Generally they are found along the margins of lakes where food is plentiful. Trout will grab any exposed crayfish when given the opportunity.

Lead Eye Crayfish, Woolly Bugger, Fleeing Crayfish

Hook Size: 4-10, 2X Long

Small crayfish often seek food and protection in heavy cover and are not often available to trout. As they grow in size, they tend to roam more in search of food and become vulnerable. When confronted by danger, a large mature male will often face it with claws outstretched, and trout are generally cautious about taking the crayfish unless it is spooked and tries to flee. Caught in the open away from shelter, females and smaller crayfish typically flee for safety, and trout often rush to grab them before they reach it. They are bottom dwellers, and that is where their imitations should be fished. Crayfish fly patterns with weighted eyes on top of their shanks sink and ride with their hook pointed upward, allowing them to slide along the bottom with fewer snags. Use a sinking or sink-tip line with the cast and retrieve method. Let the fly sink to the bottom before starting the retrieve. Mix the retrieve, taking slow, crawling strips for a foot or so, and then a number of fast foot-long strips. During the fast strips, continually twitch the rod tip for added motion to the fly. These movements mimic the crawling and fleeing crayfish. On bright days, fish deep waters near shallows with rocky bottoms or weedy cover, and during low-light times fish the shallows. Trout slam these fast stripped flies. Use a stronger tippet (2X-4X) to withstand the shock of a hitting trout and for help in casting a heavy fly.

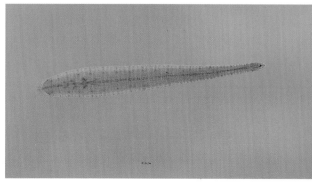

Leech

Class: Hirudinea   Size: 1-40 cm
Body Color: Shades of black, brown, and olive
J F M A M J J A S O N D   E, M, W

Leeches living in freshwater belong to one group of segmented worms from the class Hirudinea. They can reach lengths of up
to six inches or more, but normally average around four inches
long. These worms can contract enough to look like a gelatin ball
or stretch their bodies to their maximum lengths and resemble
taut rubber bands. Suckers, located at both ends of their bodies,
are used for feeding, moving, and attachment. Most species feed
by scavenging and by preying on aquatic worms, insects, crustaceans, and mollusks. A few species are bloodsuckers, normally
feeding on the blood of amphibians and fish. Their suckers also
enable them to move around like inch worms; one end hangs on
while the other end feels around or moves. When detached from
the bottom they swim with a sinuous up-and-down motion.
Individual leeches possess both sex organs. Any two can mate,
and they often produce large populations among suitable bottoms
that have plenty of cover in the forms of weeds, debris and rocks.
Leeches are light sensitive and are normally active during low-
light periods, but in areas with dense populations, they are often
seen swimming during the day. Trout take them whenever they
are available.

Bead Head Rabbit Leech, Mini Leech, Woolly Bugger
Hook Size: 2-12 3X Long

Leeches spend most of their time foraging for food on or close to bottoms with weeds, rocks, or debris in the margins of lakes. They are wanderers, and on smooth silted bottoms you can often follow their trails great distances. They are most active during the low-light conditions of morning, evening, or night and in deeper waters. Swimming leeches have a very distinctive undulating up-and-down motion. To imitate this motion use fly patterns with long flowing tails and bodies that have weight located toward the eye of the hook. The forward weight will cause the head to dip on any pause in the retrieve. This gives the fly a jigging action that matches the natural's undulating motion. Keep the fly close to the bottom; in shallow water use a floating or slow-sinking intermediate line, and for deeper waters a sink-tip or sinking line. Use the cast and retrieve and countdown method. Fish close to the bottom, and use a slow retrieve with pauses, or slowly move your rod up and down to give the fly an undulating movement during the retrieve. Vary the speed and pause time of the retrieves. Leech patterns are excellent for trolling. Use a sink-tip or sinking line that keeps the fly close to the bottom when you are trolling at a slow speed. Slowly pump the rod tip four to eight inches to add movement to the fly while trolling. Trout hit these flies hard. Use tippets strong enough to handle the strike and battle for the size of trout in the lake.

Forage Fish—Sculpin

J F M A M J J A S O N D   **E, M, W**

Forage fish in lakes include any small fish that are fed on by trout. They can be roughly divided into three groups; bottom dwellers, shallow-water dwellers and open-water schooling fish. Bottom dwellers include sculpins that live in cold, clear, rocky lakes. They are squat, mottled-brown fish up to six inches long. Slow swimmers, they seldom stray far from the bottom where they hide under rocks, logs, and weeds, and range from the lake shallows into deep water. Some shallow-water dwellers include young trout, shiners, dace, and chubs. These fish generally spend most of their time in weedy shallows during the day and at dark move a little farther out into deeper water to feed. Some of these fish swim in schools for the protection of numbers, and others move singly or in small groups. They often dart around and zip away if startled. These fish have colors that range from silver, to olive, to brown, often with additional side markings. Open-water schooling fish spend most of their time in open water, generally feeding on plankton. They include young salmon, shad, shiners, and smelt, and are typically shades of silver. They range in size from one to eight inches. These fish are usually fast swimmers and for protection gather in schools that burst apart when threatened. Trout feed on all three groups at different times.

Clouser Deep Minnow/Sculpin, Muddler Minnow, Zonker

Hook Size: 2-12, 3X Long

Sculpins are bottom dwellers that generally live in cold, clear, rocky, lakes. They swim with a short, darting motion and seldom stray far from the bottom. Use the cast and retrieve method along with the countdown method to keep the fly close to the bottom. Choose the type of fly line that matches the depth of water to be fished. The Clouser Deep Minnow/Sculpin rides hook up and is a good pattern to use in rocky areas. In weedy areas, use an unweighted Muddler Minnow fished with a sink-tip line. This combination keeps the buoyant fly floating above the weeds. Retrieve the fly with short, quick strips, adding pauses that allow the line to sink and pull the fly back toward the weeds.

Shallow-water dwellers should be imitated with a fly that matches the natural's general size and color. They hold in and around sheltered areas and typically swim with short darting movements, but flee quickly when startled. Use the cast and retrieve method with a floating or intermediate line and vary the retrieve to match the natural's movements. At dark, these fish move out into deeper water to feed, where they become more vulnerable to trout. Use a sink-tip line to cover deeper waters.

Open-water schooling fish generally move in large groups for the safety of numbers. They tend to be silver in color and live in the same water zones as trout. Use the cast and retrieve method and a fly line to match the depth to be fished. These fish are fast swimmers, so use a similar retrieve. Trolling their imitations is a good way to search open water. Also fish water around inlets and outlets where schools may gather. Trout grow large on forage fish and readily take any that are injured or stray from protection.

Ant

Order: Hymenoptera   Size: 8-20 mm
Family: Formicidae
Body Color: Black, dark brown or black/red
J F M A M J J A S O N D   E, M, W

Ants typically live in large colonies, often located in rotting wood or below ground. They have a very structured society made up of a queen, drones, and workers. There is normally only one queen, and her sole purpose is to supply the colony with eggs for its continuation. Male ants are known as drones, and they live only to mate with the queen, after which they die. Workers make up the majority of a colony's residents. They guard the colony, feed the queen and drones, and care for the eggs. Normally, ants engage in mating flights during the spring or fall. Newly-hatched, winged queens and drones leave the nest and take flight to mate. The drones gather in large swarms often high in the air; the queens fly out to choose a partner and mate. After mating, the queens return to land, lose their wings, and begin their duties. After the mating flights are over, the drones fall to earth and die, their life cycle completed. The flying drones are the winged ants that often end up on a lake's surface. When the flights occur close to or over the water, large numbers of ants often fall on the surface and trout will be there to feed selectively on them.

Black Flying Ant,
Bear's Brown No-Hackle Flying Ant, Foam Flying Ant
Hook Size: 12-18

Mating swarms normally occur high above the ground, often out of sight and far from water. Winds catch many of these ants and carry them along until they fall from the sky. Some of these swarms contain millions of ants, so there is a good chance that any open water downwind will get its share of insects. In areas of heavy timber, ants often swarm over open water, and this can produce a heavy ant fall. Most swarms occur during the spring and fall, with a smaller number spread through the summer. Some areas have well-documented ant falls, and the local fly shops normally keep tabs on them. Realistically, ant falls are not something you can count on finding. They are one of those gifts that nature drops on you occasionally, and to enjoy it you should be ready with a couple different sizes and colors of ant patterns. Ants sit low in the water. Because of this you will often see trout feeding on them before you notice the ants. Trout feeding on ants are often very selective. Collect a natural and match your fly to it. Use the cast and wait method. Try to pick out the feeding path of a trout; then cast ahead of it and let the fly sit. Floating ants collect in foam lines, off shorelines with high banks, on the lee side of points, and in wind-sheltered areas. Trout take these trapped insects gently— it may be hard to spot them from a distance—so if you find any ants on the water, keep a sharp eye for feeding trout.

Beetle

Order: Coleoptera   Size: 1-40 mm
Body Color: Black, brown, and green
J F M A M J J A S O N D   E, M, W

Beetles make up the largest order of insects. There are over 30,000 species in North America. Some are aquatic (covered in Chapter 5 under "Water Beetles"), but the majority are terrestrial. Only a small number of these are important to lake anglers. Most have distinctive, hard bodies that are oval in shape. The order's name "Coleoptera" comes from *coleo*, meaning sheath and *ptera*, meaning wing. This describes their hardened forewings that cover their hind wings and upper bodies in a protective shell when the insect is at rest. Beetles undergo complete metamorphosis—from egg, to larva, to pupa, and finally to adult. Many are considered pests for the damage they do to vegetation. Terrestrial adult beetles that can fly are the only stage available in any number to trout in lakes. They fly to expand their feeding areas or to find mates. Any that land on the water are seldom left untouched by trout.

Thompson's Foam Beetle, Hair Beetle, Foam Beetle

Hook Size: 8-18

Terrestrial beetles live around all the same areas as trout, and they periodically occur in large numbers that are often referred to as "outbreaks" or "infestations." Most of these beetles migrate to new areas by flying, and many of them end up on the surfaces of nearby lakes. These are the easiest beetles to imitate, since you'll often find one before you start fishing. Under normal conditions, beetles drop on the water often enough to keep trout interested, but not in numbers large enough to alert the angler. The infrequent swirls of trout taking unseen insects from the surface may indicate the presence of beetles, which ride low in the water and can be difficult to see. These occasional beetles are the hardest to imitate. Black beetles in various sizes are the most common, and anglers should carry a few of their imitations; add other colors as needed. It is possible to find beetles on the water at any time of the fishing season. Even if they are not present, one of their imitations is a good choice when searching the water for trout. High or cliff-lined banks and shores with overhanging foliage that have holding water next to them are always good places to try a beetle imitation. Use the cast and wait method and occasionally add a slight twitch. Rubber legs on the fly add a liveliness that even the pickiest trout cannot refuse.

Grasshopper

Order: Orthoptera   Size: 30-40 mm
Body Color: Shades of yellow, green, and brown
J F M A M J J A S O N D   E, M, W

Grasshoppers occur throughout most of North America and are common around grass and crop lands. Lacking a pupal stage, they have an incomplete metamorphosis. After the adults mate in the fall, the females lay their eggs to over-winter and hatch in the spring. The nymphs with undeveloped wings look like miniature versions of the adults. Most grasshoppers reach maturity and are able to mate by mid-summer, when their wings are fully developed. Grasshoppers are generally strong fliers. These flying adults are the ones that trout in lakes normally see on the water. There is usually no doubt when a grasshopper struggling on the water is taken by a trout, whose rise is often quick and violent.

Letort Hopper, Madam X, Foam Hopper
Hook Size: 6-12

Grasshoppers may be spread across the country, but few lakes are blessed with fishable numbers of them. The habitat around a lake is often the controlling factor in the importance of grasshoppers to anglers. Look for grassy meadows or fields next to the lake. If possible, take a short walk into the meadow. Any mature grasshoppers will make their presence known by taking flight when you get close to them. When they are found in good numbers, check the direction of the prevailing winds. This is important, since the wind must blow across the meadow into the lake. Grasshoppers are strong fliers, and without the aid of the wind few would end up in the water. Search out grassy banks that fill this requirement, as they offer the best chance to find large trout waiting for luckless hoppers to hit the water. Use a low-profile fly pattern the size and color of the natural, tied to a long leader. Trout near the shoreline are selective and spooky. This fishing is best done from the shore with the wind at your back. Keep low and sneak up on likely banks. Trout often hold in close when hoppers are available. Fish the nearest water first before extending your casts. When hoppers hit the water they start kicking their hind legs and head for shore. Try to mimic this activity, and do not overreact and break off the trout when it smashes the fly.

Fly Patterns

All flies tied by the author unless credited otherwise.

Longhorned Case Maker
(Larva)

LaFontaine Cased Caddis
(Light or Dark)
Originator: Gary LaFontaine
Hook: TMC 100, Mustad
3906B, sizes 8-14, weighted
Thread: Brown 6/0 prewaxed
Body (Light): Pale, speckled
mallard breast feathers and
lemon wooduck feathers,
wrapped together and
cut to shape
Body (Dark): Dark brown and
gray grouse feathers,
wrapped together and cut to
shape
Thorax: Pale yellow rabbit
dubbing
Legs: Dark brown and gray
grouse hackle fibers mixed
and tied down

Drifting Cased Caddis
Originator: Rene Harrop
Hook: TMC 5262, Mustad
9671, sizes 10-16, weighted
Thread: Black 6/0 prewaxed
Body: Mottled turkey wing
quill fiber, wrapped
Thorax: Green Antron dubbing
Legs: Black stiff hackle fibers,
cut
Head: Black Antron dubbing

Herl Nymph
Hook: TMC 5262, Mustad
9671, sizes 8-16, weighted
Thread: Black 6/0 prewaxed
Body: Peacock herl
Thorax: Black ostrich herl
Legs: Black hackle fibers

Longhorned Case Maker
(Pupa)

Black Sparkle Pupa
Originator: Gary LaFontaine
Hook: TMC 3796, Mustad
3906, sizes 14-16, weighted
Thread: Black 6/0 prewaxed
Underbody: Dark brown and
black Antron dubbing,
mixed
Overbody: Black Antron yarn
Legs: Dark brown hen-hackle
fibers, at sides
Head: Black rabbit dubbing

Brown Emergent Sparkle Pupa
Originator: Gary LaFontaine
Hook: TMC 3796, Mustad
3906, sizes 10-16, lightly
weighted
Thread: Dark brown 6/0 pre
waxed
Underbody: Brown Hare-Tron
dubbing
Overbody: Brown Antron
yarn

Wing: Brown deer hair
Head: Brown rabbit dubbing

White Miller
Hook: TMC 3761, Mustad
3906B, sizes 10-16
Thread: White 6/0 prewaxed
Rib: Fine flat silver tinsel
Body: White floss
Hackle: White hen hackle
Wing: White duck-wing quill

Longhorned Case Maker
(Adult)

Deer Hair Caddis
Originator: Jim Schollmeyer
Hook: TMC 900BL, Mustad
94840, sizes 10-16
Thread: Tan or black 6/0 pre
waxed
Body: Black, brown, or pale
yellow
Hackle: Dark dun, brown, or
light ginger palmered over
body, clipped on bottom
Wing: Light or dark deer hair
Note: Choose the color of the
thread, body, hackle, and
wing to match the natural.

Diving Caddis
Originator: Gary LaFontaine
Hook: TMC 3761, Mustad
3906B, sizes 10-16
Thread: Black, brown, or
white
Body: Black, brown or white
Hare-Tron
Underwing: Dark grouse, or
white hen-hackle fibers
Overwing: Clear Antron fibers

Hackle: Black, brown, or
white, sparse
Note: Choose the color of the
thread, body, hackle, and
wing to match the natural.

Parkany Deer Hair Caddis
(White)
Originator: Ken Parkany
Hook: TMC 900BL, Mustad
94845, size 10
Thread: White 6/0 prewaxed
Body: White deer hair, spun
and clipped
Wing: White deer hair
Head: Butt of wing hairs

Northern Case Maker
(Larva)

Hazel's Cased Caddis
Originator: John Hazel
Hook: TMC 300, Mustad
79580, sizes 6-10, weighted
Thread: Black 6/0 prewaxed
Rib: Fine copper wire
Body: Peacock herl
Hackle: Furnace saddle-hackle,
palmered over body and
clipped
Thorax: Cream rabbit dubbing
Head: Black goat dubbing,
picked out

Cased Caddis
Originator: George Bodmer
Hook: TMC 5262, Mustad
9671, sizes 6-10, weighted
Thread: Black 6/0 prewaxed
Rib: Copper Wire
Underbody: Tapered dark
brown yarn

Overbody: Brown and black
hackle, palmered over
underbody and clipped
Head: Black ostrich herl

Medium Cased Caddis
Hook: TMC 300, Mustad
79580, sizes 6-10, weighted
Thread: Black 6/0 prewaxed
Underbody: Silver tinsel che
nille
Body: Muskrat fur
Head: Black ostrich herl

Northern Case Maker
(Pupa)

Deep Sparkle Pupa
Originator: Gary LaFontaine
Hook: TMC 3761, Mustad
3906B, sizes 6-10, weighted
Thread: Black 6/0 prewaxed
Underbody: Brown or ginger
Antron dubbing to match
natural
Overbody: Tan Antron yarn
Legs: Grouse hackle fibers
Head: Brown rabbit fur

Emergent Sparkle Pupa
Originator: Gary LaFontaine
Hook: TMC 100, Mustad
94845, sizes 6-10
Thread: Black 6/0 prewaxed
Underbody: Brown or ginger
Antron dubbing to match
natural
Overbody: Tan Antron yarn
Wing: Dark deer hair
Head: Brown rabbit dubbing

Sparkle Caddis Pupa
Originator: Gary Borger
Hook: TMC 3761, Mustad
3906B, sizes 6-10, weighted
Thread: 6/0 Black prewaxed
Body: Ginger to brown Antron
dubbing to match natural
Thorax: Antron brown to
ginger, cut twice length of
hook shank, then dubbed
and picked out
Hackle: Brown hen hackle

Northern Case Maker
(Adult)

Canoe Fly
Hook: TMC 900BL, Mustad
94840, sizes 4-10
Thread: Tan 6/0
Body: Ginger to brown Antron
dubbing to match natural
Wing: Deer hair
Head: Butts of wing

Deer Hair Caddis
Originator: Jim Schollmeyer
Hook: TMC 900BL, Mustad
94840, sizes 4-10
Thread: Tan 6/0 prewaxed
Body: Ginger to brown
Hare-tron dubbing to match
natural
Hackle: Ginger or brown
palmered over body, bottom
clipped
Wing: Deer hair
Head: Butts of wing

Elk Hair Caddis
Originator: Al Troth

Hook: TMC 100, Mustad
94845, sizes 4-10
Thread: Tan 6/0 prewaxed
Rib: Fine gold wire
Body: Ginger to brown dub
bing to match natural
Hackle: Ginger hackle
palmered over body
Wing: Light elk hair
Head: Butts of wing

Giant Case Maker
(Larva)

Lake Peeking Caddis
Hook: TMC 5263, Mustad
9672, sizes 4-8, weighted
Thread: Black 6/0 prewaxed
Rib: Copper wire
Body: Natural hare's ear
dubbing
Thorax: Pale yellow rabbit
dubbing
Legs: Brown hen-hackle fibers
Head: Dark brown rabbit
dubbing

Hazel's Cased Caddis
Originator: John Hazel
Hook: TMC 300, Mustad
79580, sizes 4-8, weighted
Thread: Black 6/0 prewaxed
Rib: Fine copper wire
Body: Peacock herl
Hackle: Furnace saddle-hackle,
palmered over body, and
clipped
Thorax: Cream rabbit dubbing
Head: Black goat dubbing,
picked out

Caddis Larva
Originator: Gary LaFontaine
Hook: TMC 200R, sizes 6-10,
weighted
Thread: Black 6/0 prewaxed
Rib: Stripped brown hackle
stem
Body: Pale yellow Antron
dubbing
Thorax: Brown Antron
dubbing
Legs: Brown grouse hackle
fibers

Giant Case Maker
(Pupa)

Sedge Pupa
Hook: TMC 5262, Mustad
9672, sizes 4-10, weighted
Thread: Brown 6/0 prewaxed
Body: Brown, green, or yellow
to match natural
Wings: Gray duck primaries
Legs: Pheasant rump fibers
Head: Brown rabbit dubbing

Deep Sparkle Pupa
Originator: Gary LaFontaine
Hook: TMC 3761, Mustad
3906B, sizes 4-10, weighted
Thread: Black 6/0 prewaxed
Underbody: Brown, gray,
green, or yellow Antron
dubbing to match natural
Overbody: Tan Antron yarn
Legs: Grouse hackle fibers
Head: Brown rabbit fur

Sparkle Caddis Pupa
Originator: Gary Borger

Hook: TMC 3761, Mustad
3906B, sizes 4-10, weighted
Thread: 6/0 Black prewaxed
Body: Brown, gray, green, or
yellow Antron dubbing to
match natural
Thorax: Brown to ginger
Antron yarn cut twice length
of hook shank, then dubbed
and picked out
Hackle: Brown hen hackle

Giant Case Maker
(Adult)

Traveling Sedge
Originator: Karl Poulson
Hook: TMC 2302, Mustad
9671, sizes 4-10
Thread: Black 6/0 prewaxed
Tail: Tan calf tail
Rib: Brown hackle, clipped
short
Body: Brown, gray, green, or
yellow Antron dubbing to
match natural
Wing: Deer hair
Hackle: Ginger and grizzly
mixed, bottom clipped

Tom Thumb
Hook: TMC 2302, Mustad
9671, sizes 4-10
Thread: Black 6/0 prewaxed
Tail: Deer hair
Body: Deer hair or dubbing to
match natural
Wing: Deer hair tips from
body

Diving Caddis
Originator: Gary LaFontaine

Hook: TMC 3761, Mustad
3906B, sizes 4-10, weighted
Thread: Black 6/0 prewaxed
Body: Brown, gray, green, or
yellow Antron dubbing to
match natural
Underwing: Grouse hackle
fibers
Overwing: Clear Antron fibers
Hackle: Brown or ginger,
sparse

Speckle-wing Quill
(Nymph)

**CDC *Callibaetis* Floating
Nymph/Emerger**
Originator: Rene Harrop
Hook: TMC 5230, Mustad
94833, sizes 12-16
Thread: Tan 6/0 prewaxed
Tail: Woodduck flank fibers
Rib: Fine copper wire
Body: Tan rabbit dubbing
Legs: Brown partridge hackle
fibers
Wing: White CDC feathers,
short
Thorax: Tan rabbit dubbing

Timberline
Originator: Randall Kaufmann
Hook: TMC 2302, Mustad
3906B, sizes 12-18, weighted
Thread: Tan 6/0 prewaxed
Tail: Ringneck pheasant tail
fibers
Rib: Fine copper wire
Body: Blend equal parts of
beaver fur and gray goat or
hare's ear
Wingcase: Ringneck pheasant

tail fibers
Thorax: Same as body
Legs: Ringneck pheasant tail
fiber tips, from wingcase

Marabou P.T. Nymph
Originator: Jim Schollmeyer
Hook: TMC 3761, Mustad
3906B, sizes 12-16, weighted
Thread: Brown, tan or olive to
match natural, 8/0 pre-
waxed
Tail: Dyed or natural pheasant
tail fibers, to match natural,
flared
Rib: Fine copper wire
Body: Dyed marabou, color to
match natural, two to four
strands twisted in dubbing
loop and wrapped
Wingcase: Pheasant tail fibers,
same color as tail
Thorax: Peacock herl
Legs: Tips of pheasant tail
fibers from wingcase

Speckle-wing Quill
(Dun)

Callibaetis Comparadun
Tier: Ted Leeson
Hook: TMC 900BL, Mustad
94845, sizes 12-18
Thread: Olive 6/0 prewaxed
Wing: Deer body hair, flared
in a 160-degree arc
Tail: Ginger hackle fibers, split
Body: Light olive-tan dubbing

Speckled-wing Parachute
Originator: Pret Frazier
Tier: Ted Leeson

Hook: TMC 100, Mustad
94845, sizes 12-18
Thread: 6/0 prewaxed, match
body color
Tail: Micro Fibetts, to match
natural
Body: Rabbit dubbing, to
match natural
Wing: Mallard flank, trimmed
to shape
Hackle: Neck hackle, to match
natural, parachute style

Natural Dun *Callibaetis*
Originator: Richard Bunse
Tier: Richard Bunse
Hook: Mustad 94838, sizes 12-18
Thread: Brown 6/0 prewaxed
Tail: Beaver fur guard hair
fibers
Body: Packing foam, colored
with a waterproof marking
pen, light gray or tan
Wing: Natural gray deer hair
and teal flank feather fibers

Speckle-wing Quill
(Spinner)

Gulper Special
Originator: Al Troth
Tier: Ted Leeson
Hook: TMC 100, Mustad
94845, sizes 12-18
Thread: Brown 6/0 prewaxed
Tail: Grizzly hackle fibers
Body: Dark beaver fur
Wing: White or dun poly yarn
Hackle: Grizzly hackle,
parachute style

Bunse's *Callibaetis* Spinner
Originator: Richard Bunse
Tier: Richard Bunse
Hook: Mustad 94838, sizes 12-18
Thread: Brown 6/0 prewaxed
Tail: Beaver fur guard hair fibers
Body: Packing foam, colored with a waterproof marking pen, light gray or tan
Wing: Clear Antron yarn and teal flank feather fibers tied spent

CDC *Callibaetis* Biot Spinner
Originator: Rene Harrop
Tier: Ted Leeson
Hook: TMC 5230, Mustad 94833, sizes 12-16
Thread: Tan 6/0 prewaxed
Tail: Ginger cock-hackle fibers
Wings: White CDC feathers with brown Z-Lon over the top
Abdomen: Brown goose biot, wrapped
Thorax: Tan rabbit dubbing

Gray Drake
(Nymph)

Marabou Nymph
Hook: TMC 2302, Mustad 3906B, sizes 6-10, lightly weighted
Thread: Gray 6/0 prewaxed
Tail: Gray marabou, short
Rib: Fine oval silver tinsel
Body: Gray rabbit dubbing
Wing: Gray marabou
Wingcase: Gray Z-Lon

Thorax: Gray rabbit dubbing
Legs: Speckled guinea-hackle fibers

Black Drake
Originator: Polly Rosborough
Hook: TMC 5263, Mustad 38491, sizes 6-10, lightly weighted
Thread: Gray 6/0 prewaxed
Tail: Guinea-hackle fibers
Body: Beaver belly fur, with guard hairs
Wingcase: Black ostrich herl, short
Legs: Guinea-hackle fibers

Marabou P.T. Nymph
Originator: Jim Schollmeyer
Hook: TMC 3761, Mustad 3906B, sizes 8-12, weighted
Thread: Brown, tan olive or gray to match natural, 8/0 prewaxed
Tail: Dyed or natural pheasant tail fibers, to match natural, flared
Rib: Fine copper wire
Body: Dyed marabou, color to match natural, two to four strands twisted in dubbing loop and wrapped
Wingcase: Pheasant tail fibers, same color as tail
Thorax: Peacock herl
Legs: Tips of pheasant tail fibers from wingcase

Gray Drake
(Spinner)

Gray Drake Parachute
Originator: Jim Schollmeyer
Hook: TMC 900BL, Mustad
94845, sizes 10-12
Thread: Brown 6/0 prewaxed
Tail: Dun hackle fibers, split
Body: Dark reddish-brown or
grayish-brown dubbing to
match natural
Wing: Gray poly yarn, short
Hackle: Light dun hackle,
parachute style

Spent Mayfly Gray Drake
Hook: TMC 900BL, Mustad
94845, sizes 8-12
Thread: Gray 6/0 prewaxed
Tail: Gray Micro Fibetts
Hackle: Light dun hackle,
oversized, wrapped and
split spent
Body: Dark reddish-brown or
grayish-brown dubbing to
match natural

Clear Wing Spinner
Hook: TMC 900BL, Mustad
94845, sizes 8-12
Thread: Brown 6/0 prewaxed
Tail: Dark dun hackle fibers
Wing: Clear Antron
Body: Dark reddish-brown or
grayish-brown dubbing to
match natural

Big Yellow May
(Nymph)

Hexagenia **Wiggle Nymph**
Originators: Doug Swisher
and Carl Richards
Hooks: Thorax, Mustad 3906,
size 6; abdomen, Mustad
9674, size 8, weighted
Thread: Tan 6/0 prewaxed
Tail: Tan ostrich herl
Rib: Copper wire
Abdomen: Olive-brown
dubbing; four strands of
brown ostrich herl along
sides
Thorax: Olive-brown dubbing
Wingcase: Dark mottled
turkey tail segment
Legs: Light brown partridge
hackle fibers
Note: Cut the hook behind the
tails after tying abdomen.
Use 12 pound leader
material to form connection
loop and secure it with tight
thread wraps covered with
Super Glue.

Streamlined Nymph
Hook: TMC 5263, Mustad
9672, size 4, weighted
Thread: Tan 6/0 prewaxed
Tail: Tan ostrich herl
Rib: Gold wire
Abdomen: Olive-brown
dubbing, four strands of
gray ostrich herl along sides
tied down with rib
Thorax: Olive-brown dubbing
Wing case: Dark mottled
turkey tail segment

Legs: Light brown partridge
hackle fibers

Strip Nymph
Originator: Gray Borger
Hook: TMC 3769, Mustad
3906, size 6, weighted
Thread: Tan 6/0 prewaxed
Abdomen: Strip of tanned
hide with fur intact, 3/16
inch wide, extended
Thorax: Tan dubbing
Legs: Rabbit guard hairs
added to thorax dubbing,
clipped on bottom
Covert: Peacock herl

Big Yellow May
(Dun)

Bunse's *Hex* Dun
Originator: Richard Bunse
Tier: Richard Bunse
Hook: Mustad 94838, sizes 8-10
Thread: Black 6/0 prewaxed
Tail: Beaver fur guard hair
fibers
Body: Packing foam, colored
yellow-olive with a
waterproof marking pen,
extended
Wing: Light colored deer hair

Hair Wing Dun
Originator: Gary Borger
Hook: TMC 100, Mustad
94845, sizes 6-10
Thread: Dark Brown 3/0 pre
waxed
Tail: Pheasant tail barbs
Body: Yellow-olive deer hair,
extended

Thorax: Dubbing to match
body
Wing: Natural gray deer hair

Clark's Big Yellow Mayfly
Parachute
Originator: Lee Clark
Tier: Lee Clark
Hook: TMC 5262, Mustad
9671, sizes 8-10
Thread: Yellow 6/0 prewaxed
Body: Flat gold tinsel, with
yellow-brown macramé
yarn, combed and twisted
Wing: Dyed yellow deer hair
Hackle: Dyed yellow grizzly
hackle, parachute style

Big Yellow May
(Spinner)

Hair Wing Spinner
Hook: TMC 100, Mustad
94845, sizes 8-10
Thread: Brown 6/0 prewaxed
Tail: Pheasant tail fibers, ends
of extended body
Body: Yellow deer hair
extended over pheasant tail
Wing: Light deer hair, tied
spent and topped with Pearl
Krystal Flash

Clark's Big Yellow Mayfly
Spinner
Originator: Lee Clark
Tier: Lee Clark
Hook: TMC 5363, Mustad
9672, size 10
Thread: Yellow 6/0 prewaxed
Underbody: Gold tinsel
Wing: Gray polypropylene

macramé yarn, 2 strands
combed, tied spent
Overbody: Gold polypropylene macramé yarn, three
strands, combed and twisted
Head: Butt ends of overbody,
2 strands

Bunse's *Hex* Spinner
Originator: Richard Bunse
Tier: Richard Bunse
Hook: TMC 100, Mustad
94845, sizes 8-10
Thread: Yellow 6/0 prewaxed
Tail: Micro Fibetts
Body: Ethafoam sheeting
colored yellow
Wing: White polypropylene
macramé yarn, 2 strands,
combed, tied spent

Trico
(Dun)

CDC Trico Emerger
Tier: Ted Leeson
Hook: TMC 100, Mustad
94845, sizes 18-22
Thread: Olive 8/0 prewaxed
Tail: Tan Z-Lon, sparse
Abdomen: Olive dubbing
Wing: Dun CDC feather
Thorax: Dark brown dubbing

Gulper Special
Originator: Al Troth
Tier: Ted Leeson
Hook: TMC 100, Mustad
94845, sizes 18-20
Thread: Brown 8/0 prewaxed
Tail: Grizzly hackle fibers

Body: Dark gray dubbing
Wing: White polypro yarn
Hackle: Grizzly hackle,
parachute style

Little Olive Parachute
Tier: Ted Leeson
Hook: TMC 100, Mustad
94845, sizes 18-22
Thread: Olive 8/0 prewaxed
Tail: Light dun hackle fibers,
split
Body: Olive dubbing
Wing: Dun polypro yarn
Hackle: Light dun hackle,
parachute style

Trico
(Spinner)

Trico Parachute
Tier: Ted Leeson
Hook: TMC 101, Mustad
94859, sizes 20-24
Thread: White 8/0 prewaxed
Tail: Grizzly hackle fibers
Body: White thread
Wing: Light gray poly yarn,
short
Thorax: Black dubbing
Hackle: Grizzly dun hackle,
parachute style

Krystal Flash Spinner
Originator: George Harvey
Hook: TMC 101, Mustad
94859, sizes 18-22
Thread: 8/0 light gray pre
waxed
Tail: Clear or gray Micro
Fibetts

Abdomen: Light gray dubbing
Underwing: Clear Antron or white CDC
Overwing: Pearl Krystal Flash
Thorax: Black dubbing

Trico Poly Spinner
Tier: Ted Leeson
Hook: TMC 101, Mustad 94859, sizes 18-24
Thread: Black 8/0 prewaxed
Tail: Dark dun Micro Fibetts, split
Abdomen: White dubbing
Thorax: Black dubbing
Wings: White poly yarn

Midge
(Larva)

Brassie
Originator: Gene Lynch
Hook: TMC 5262, Mustad 9671, sizes 10-16
Thread: Black 6/0 prewaxed
Body: Copper wire, also in red, green, or brown
Thorax: Gray dubbing, with guard hairs

Krystal Flash Midge
Originator: Rick Hafele
Hook: TMC 5262, Mustad 9671, sizes 10-16
Thread: Dark brown 6/0 pre waxed
Body: Krystal Flash, black, green, red, or copper, two to four strands twisted and wrapped
Head: Dark brown rabbit with guard hairs

Swannundaze Midge
Originator: Boyd Aigner
Hook: TMC 2312, sizes 12-18
Thread: Olive 6/0 prewaxed
Gills: White poly yarn
Abdomen: Swannundaze, black, brown olive or red
Thorax: Peacock herl

Midge
(Pupa)

Seed Bead Midge Pupa
Originator: Joe Warren
Tier: Joe Warren
Hook: Mustad AC8025BR, size 12
Thread: Black 8/0
Tail: Black Antron yarn, sparse, tip of black goose biot over top
Body: Seed Beads size 11/0 (by Gick Craft), 5 root-beer colored, green, or black,
Head: Black ostrich herl

Suspender Midge
Originator: Doug Jorgensen
Hook: TMC 900BL, Mustad 94840, sizes 12-18
Thread: Black 6/0 or 8/0 pre waxed
Tail: White closed cell packing foam, cut into a strip and tied in to form tail, underbody and head
Rib: Fine gold wire
Body: Dubbing, biot, or foam, color to match natural
Thorax: Peacock herl

TDC
Originator: Richard Thompson
Hook: TMC 5262, Mustad 9671, sizes 10-16, weight at rear optional
Thread: Black 6/0 prewaxed
Rib: Fine flat silver tinsel
Body: Black dubbing or color to match natural
Thorax: Black dubbing
Head: White ostrich herl

Midge
(Adult)

Parachute Midge Emerger
Originators: Gary Willmott and Scott Sachez
Hook: TMC 101, Mustad 94859, sizes 14-18
Thread: Black 8/0 prewaxed
Body: Peacock colored Antron dubbing or color to match natural
Rib: Rainbow Krystal Flash
Wing: White Antron
Hackle: Grizzly or dun, parachute style

Griffith's Gnat
Originator: George Griffith
Hook: TMC 101, Mustad 94859, sizes 16-20
Thread: Olive 8/0 prewaxed
Rib: Fine gold wire
Body: Peacock herl
Hackle: Grizzly hackle, palmered over body

CDC Midge Adult
Originator: Rene Harrop

Hook: TMC 5230, Mustad 94833, sizes 14-20
Thread: Black 8/0 prewaxed
Body: Stripped black ostrich herl, or color to match natural
Wing: White CDC feather
Legs: Black CDC feathers
Thorax: Black dubbing

Damselfly
(Nymphs)

Henry's Damselfly Nymph
Originator: Henry Hoffman
Tier: Henry Hoffman
Hook: TMC 200R, Mustad 9672, sizes 8-12
Thread: Olive 6/0 prewaxed
Eyes: Mono, burnt to shape
Tail: Olive Chickabou tips
Rib: Brass wire
Body: The rest of the Chickabou tail feather, twisted and wrapped
Legs: Chickabou tips or fluff
Thorax: Olive dubbing to match body color

Warren's Damsel
Originator: Gary Warren
Tier: Gary Warren
Hook: TMC 200R, sizes 8-12
Thread: Olive 6/0 prewaxed
Tail: Olive or brown marabou
Body: Olive or brown marabou from tail wrapped forward
Wingcase: Olive or brown duck quill, dull side up
Eyes: Mono nymph eyes

Brown Eyed Damsel
Originator: Jim Cope
Tier: Jim Cope
Hook: TMC 200R, sizes 8-12
Thread: Brown 6/0 prewaxed
Tail: Brown pheasant tail
Rib: Dyed brown paint brush bristles, or clear mono
Body: Brown rabbit dubbing
Wingcase: Dyed brown paint brush bristles, clipped; or brown ringneck pheasant tail fibers, clipped
Legs: Dyed brown pheasant tail
Eyes: Mono nymph eyes
Head: Brown rabbit dubbing
Note: Jim dyes synthetic paint brushes with Rit dyes in browns and olives to match the color of the natural

Damselfly
(Adult)

Braided Butt Damsel
Originators: Bob Pelzl, Gary Borger
Hook: TMC 900BL, Mustad 94845, sizes 10-12
Thread: Blue 6/0 prewaxed, or to match body color
Body: Braided monofilament (leader butt), colored with waterproof marker to match natural
Thorax: Dubbing color to match natural
Hackle Post: Yarn color to match natural
Hackle: Light dun wrapped parachute style

Shellback: Hackle post pulled forward
Head: Shellback butts

Parachute Damsel, Blue
Hook: TMC 5212, Mustad 94831, sizes 8-12
Thread: Black 6/0 prewaxed
Rib: Black thread
Body: Medium blue bucktail, tied extended
Hackle: Light dun, wrapped parachute style
Shellback: Medium blue bucktail, twisted
Head: Shellback butts

Shewey's Adult Damsel
Originator: John Shewey
Hook: TMC 900BL, Mustad 94845, sizes 10-12
Thread: Black 6/0 prewaxed
Body: Blue bucktail, tied extended
Rib: Black tying thread
Head: Bullet head from butts of extended body
Wing Post: Butts from head
Wings: Grizzly or blue dun hackle tips (optional)
Hackle: Grizzly or blue dun, parachute style

Dragonfly
(Nymph—Climber)

Rabbit Strip Dragon
Originator: Jim Schollmeyer
Hook: TMC 300, Mustad 36620, size 6, weighted
Thread: Brown 3/0 prewaxed

Abdomen: Brown or olive
  crosscut rabbit strip
Thorax: Brown or olive
  dubbing
Legs: Brown rubber legs
Eyes: Lead or mono

Bottom Walker
Originator: Alf Davy
Hook: TMC 300, Mustad
  79580, sizes 6-10
Thread: Brown 3/0 prewaxed
Body: Deer hair, spun and
  clipped to shape, color with
  waterproof pen to match
  natural
Wingcase: Peacock herl
Legs: Tips of peacock wing
  case, thin
Hackle: Black moose mane,
  tied down as beard past
  hook point

All Rounder Dragonfly Nymph
Originator: John Barr
Hook: TMC 5262, Mustad
  9671, sizes 4-8
Thread: Brown 3/0 prewaxed
Tail: Clump of black marabou
Rib: 3X mono
Back: Plastic strip cut from
  Zip-loc bag
Body: Brown/olive dubbing,
  color top of body with black
  waterproof marker
Legs: Black hen-hackle, poor
  grade
Eyes: Umpqua mono nymph
  eyes, small

Dragonfly
(Nymph—Sprawler)

Henry's Dragon Nymph
Originator: Henry Hoffman
Tier: Henry Hoffman
Hook: TMC 5263, Mustad
  9672, sizes 6-10
Thread: Olive or brown 6/0
  prewaxed
Eyes: Brass or lead
Tail: Olive or brown
  Chickabou tips
Rib: Brass wire
Body: Olive or brown
  Chickabou wrapped and
  clipped to shape
Legs: Chickabou tips
Wing: Turkey wing cut to
  shape
Head: Dubbing, color to
  match body

Gierach Dragon
Originator: John Gierach
Hook: TMC 200R, sizes 8-12,
  weighted
Thread: Brown 6/0 prewaxed
Eyes: Monofilament
Rib: Flat gold tinsel
Abdomen: Olive-brown
  dubbing
Legs: Brown partridge—
  divided; dark brown deer-
  bearded; turkey tail—cut
  short
Head: Olive-brown dubbing

Janssen Dragon
Originator: Hal Janssen
Hook: TMC 5263, Mustad
  9672, sizes 6-10, weighted

Thread: Olive 6/0 prewaxed
Abdomen: Marabou, tied in clumps around hook and clipped to shape, color to match natural
Eyes: Red 45 pound Amnesia or monofilament
Legs: Dark turkey tail, three pairs, shorter toward front
Thorax: Marabou, spun clip pings from abdomen
Wingcase: Peacock eye herl tips
Head: Same as thorax

Water Boatmen

Corixid
Hook: TMC 3761, Mustad 3906B, sizes 14-18, lightly weighted in front
Thread: Dark Olive 6/0 prewaxed
Body: Light tan to olive Hare-Tron, to match substrate, picked out

Boatman
Originator: Jim Schollmeyer
Hook: TMC 3671, Mustad 3906B, sizes 14-16, lightly weighted in front
Thread: Tan 6/0 prewaxed
Eyes: Red Amnesia 15 pound
Shellback: Light or dark hen feather fibers to match natural
Abdomen: Tan, brown, or olive Hair-tron, color to match natural mixed with white Antron, picked out
Legs: Goose biots or rubber legs, color to match body
Thorax: Hare-tron dubbing, same as body

Sparkle Boatman
Originator: Gary Borger
Hook: TMC 3761, Mustad 3609B, sizes 12-18, lightly weighted in front
Thread: Tan 6/0 prewaxed
Abdomen: Dubbing and Antron yarn to match natural
Thorax: Mixed dubbing to match natural and Antron yarn cut to twice length of hook shank, spun in dubbing loop
Hackle: Soft hen hackle to match body

Predacious Diving Beetle
(Larva)

Creeper
Hook: TMC 5263, Mustad 9672, sizes 6-12, weighted
Thread: Brown 3/0 prewaxed
Body: Deer hair, spun and clipped to shape, or colored olive with waterproof marker to match natural
Legs: Brown hen fibers tied to sides
Beard: Black moose mane, tied down past hook point, then clipped

Simulator
Originator: Randall Kaufmann
Hook: TMC 5263, Mustad 9672, sizes 6-12, weighted

Thread: 6/0 prewaxed, to match body
Tail: Turkey biot, color to match body
Rib: Copper wire
Hackle: Saddle hackle to match body, palmered and clipped
Body: Olive, brown, or tan dubbing to match color of natural

Woolly Worm
Hook: TMC 5263, Mustad 9672, sizes 6-12, weighted
Thread: To match body color
Hackle: Olive or brown, palmered
Body: Olive, brown, or tan chenille

Predacious Diving Beetle
(Adult)

Swimming Beetle
Originator: Jim Schollmeyer
Hook: TMC 5262, Mustad 9671, sizes 4-12, lightly weighted in front
Thread: Dark Brown 6/0 pre waxed
Weed Guard: Clear mono-filament, 8 or 10 pound
Tail: White Antron, sparse
Shellback: Back or dark brown Antron yarn
Abdomen: Dark brown Hare-Tron dubbing
Legs: Dark brown rubber legs
Thorax: Dark brown Hare-Tron dubbing

Soft Hackle
Hook: TMC 3761, Mustad 3906B, sizes 4-12, weighted
Thread: Dark brown 6/0 prewaxed
Rib: Silver tinsel
Body: Dark brown or black Hare-Tron dubbing
Hackle: Brown or black hen hackle

Deep Sparkle Pupa
Originator: Gary LaFontaine
Hook: TMC 3761, Mustad 3906B, sizes 8-12, weighted
Thread: Black 6/0 prewaxed
Overbody: Dark brown or black Antron yarn
Underbody: Brown or gray Antron dubbing
Legs: Mallard flank fibers
Head: Dubbing same as underbody

Alderfly
(Adult)

Deer Hair Caddis
Originator: Jim Schollmeyer
Hook: TMC 900BL, Mustad 94845, sizes 8-14
Thread: Dark brown 6/0 pre waxed
Hackle: Dark blue dun, palmered over body, bottom clipped even with hook point
Body: Dark brown Hare-Tron
Wing: Dark natural dun deer hair
Head: Butts of wing

Alder
Hook: TMC 3761, Mustad 3906B, sizes 8-14
Thread: Black 6/0 prewaxed
Tag: Fine flat gold tinsel
Body: Peacock herl
Hackle: Black hen hackle
Wing: Dark turkey wing quill

Morse's Alder Fly
Hook: TMC 3761, Mustad 3906B, sizes 8-14
Thread: Black 6/0 prewaxed
Body: Dyed black squirrel tail, wrapped
Shellback: Dyed back squirrel tail, three segments
Wing: Dyed black squirrel tail

Scuds

Scud
Hook: TMC 2457, sizes 6-22
Thread: Match color of natural
Tail: Webby dyed hackle to match body
Rib: Fine gold wire
Shellback: Plastic cut from a Zip-loc bag
Body: Antron dubbing, tan, olive, or gray, color to match natural
Antennae: Same as tail

Gammarus-Hyallella **Scud**
Originator: Randall Kaufmann
Hook: TMC 200R, sizes 10-18, weighted
Thread: Match natural
Tail: Hackle to match natural
Rib: Clear monofilament
Shellback: Clear plastic

Body: Blend of Hare-Tron and goat, picked out on bottom, color tan or olive to match natural
Antennae: Hackle, same as tail

Ostrich Scud
Originator: Fred Arbona
Hook: TMC 200R, sizes 12-18
Thread: Olive or tan to match natural
Rib: Clear monofilament
Shellback: Clear plastic
Body: Ostrich herl, olive or tan to match natural

Crayfish

Lead Eyed Crayfish
Hook: TMC 5263, Mustad 9672, sizes 6-12
Thread: Brown 6/0 prewaxed
Eyes: Brass or lead eyes, tied on top of hook shank at bend
Shellback: Brown Swiss Straw, tied in on bottom of hook shank
Thorax: Brown Seal Clone
Claws: Red squirrel tail, tied in on bottom of hook shank behind eyes, divided
Rib: Copper wire, tied behind eyes, wrapped over shell back and body
Body: Brown Seal Clone, picked out
Tail: Butt end of shellback

Woolly Bugger
Hook: TMC 5263, Mustad 9672, sizes 6-12, weighted
Thread: Brown or olive 6/0 prewaxed

Tail: Brown or olive marabou
Body: Brown or olive chenille
Hackle: Brown or olive, palmered

Fleeing Crayfish
Originator: Gary Borger
Hook: TMC 5262, Mustad 9671, sizes 4-10
Thread: Brown 3/0 prewaxed
Eyes: Chrome-plated lead eyes, tied on top of hook shank
Tail: Pale olive green marabou, length of hook shank
Body: Rusty brown fur, pale tan yarn strand added to dubbing loop to form shaggy body
Hackle: Bronze body feather from pheasant, leave on fluff
Fur Strip: Rusty brown rabbit, threaded on the hook with bare side up

Leeches

Bead Head Rabbit Leech
Hook: TMC 300, Mustad 79580, sizes 2-8, weighted
Thread: Brown, black, or olive to match body, 6/0 prewaxed
Head: Brass or black bead, size to match hook
Tail: Brown, black, or olive rabbit fur strip, length of hook shank, darken leather with waterproof marker
Body: Cross-cut rabbit strip same color as tail.

Optional: Krystal Flash topping on tail and body, 2 strands each of red and black

Mini Leech
Originator: Randall Kaufmann
Hook: TMC 200R, sizes 6-12
Head: Black or brass bead, optional
Thread: Color to match body, 6/0 prewaxed
Tail: Red, maroon, olive, brown, or black marabou, with 6 to 8 strands of matching or pearl Krystal Flash
Abdomen: Angora goat or Crystal Seal to match tail color, twisted in loop formed from Krystal Flash of matching color

Woolly Bugger
Hook: TMC 300, Mustad 79580, sizes 2-10, weighted
Thread: Black, brown, or olive to match body color 6/0 pre waxed
Tail: Black, brown, or olive marabou, with 4 to 6 strands of pearl Krystal Flash on each side
Body: Black, brown, or olive chenille, dubbing or yarn
Rib: Fine copper or silver wire
Hackle: Color to match body, palmered over body

Forage Fish

**Clouser Deep
Minnow / Sculpin**
Originator: Bob Clouser
Hook: TMC 3761, Mustad
3906B, sizes 2-6
Thread: Brown 3/0 monocord
Eyes: Lead eyes, painted red
with black pupils
Lower Wing: Pale-orange
bucktail or red squirrel tail
Middle Wing: Gold Krystal
Flash
Upper Wing: Rusty-brown
bucktail

Muddler Minnow
Originator: Dan Gapen
Hook: TMC 5263, Mustad
9672, sizes 4-14
Thread: Black 6/0 prewaxed
Tail: Mottled brown turkey
wing
Body: Flat gold tinsel
Underwing: Mottled brown
turkey wing
Overwing: Brown and white
squirrel or calf tail
Collar: Deer hair tips from
head
Head: Flared deer hair, cut to
shape

Zonker
Originator: Dan Byford
Hook: TMC 300, Mustad 9674,
sizes 2-10
Thread: Black 6/0 prewaxed
Tail: Unraveled silver Mylar
piping, from end of body
Body: Silver Mylar piping,

tied down in back with red
thread
Hackle: Grizzly hen hackle
Wing: Natural gray tan
stripped rabbit fur, tied
down with the red thread at
end of body

Ant

Black Flying Ant
Hook: TMC 900BL, Mustad
94845, sizes 12-18
Thread: Black 6/0 prewaxed
Abdomen: Black Antron
dubbing
Wings: Light blue dun hen-
hackle tips
Hackle: Black, two or three
wraps, clipped on bottom
Thorax: Black Antron dubbing

**Bear's Brown No-Hackle
Flying Ant**
Originator: Bear McKinney
Hook: TMC 900BL, Mustad
94845, sizes 12-10
Thread: Dark brown 8/0 pre
waxed
Body: Fine poly dubbing, rust
or dark brown
Wing: White Antron yarn
Legs: Dark brown Antron
yarn

Foam Flying Ant
Originator: Jim Schollmeyer
Hook: TMC 900BL, Mustad
95845, sizes 12-14
Thread: Color to match body
8/0 prewaxed

Abdomen: White packing or ethafoam, tied at rear of hook then fold forward to form body

Body Color: Black, dark brown, or cinnamon, color with waterproof marker before installing wing and hackle

Wing: White Antron yarn

Hackle: Color to match body

Head: Foam from body continued forward

Beetle

Thompson's Foam Beetle

Originator: Ken Thompson

Hook: TMC 900BL, Mustad 94845, sizes 8-18

Thread: Color to match natural, 6/0 or 8/0 to match hook size

Body: Antron dubbing, color to match natural

Legs: Cock hackle, one size smaller than normal, palmered over front half of body, clipped bottom

Shellback: Foam strip, color with waterproof marker to match natural

Hair Beetle

Originator: Jack Dennis

Hook: TMC 900BL, Mustad 94845, sizes 8-18

Thread: Black 6/0 prewaxed

Body: Black dubbing or color to match natural

Rib: Pearl Krystal Flash, 2 strands

Legs: Krystal Flash, 6-8 strands, root beer or black

Indicator: Orange Glo Bug yarn

Foam Beetle

Hook: TMC 900BL, Mustad 95845, sizes 8-14

Thread: Black 6/0 prewaxed

Shellback: Black foam (evazote)

Body: Back dubbing

Legs: Black rubber hackle

Indicator: Red yarn

Head: Butt from shellback

Grasshopper

Letort Hopper

Originator: Ed Shenk

Hook: TMC 5212, Mustad 94831, sizes 8-14

Thread: Gray 6/0 prewaxed

Body: Yellow dubbing

Wing: Mottled turkey wing quill

Overwing: Natural deer hair

Head: Butt ends of wing clipped to shape

Madam-X

Originator: Doug Swisher

Hook: TMC 5212, Mustad 94831, sizes 8-12

Thread: Yellow 6/0 prewaxed

Tail: Deer hair

Body: Yellow floss or Antron yarn to match natural's color

Wing: Deer hair

Head: Deer hair, tied forward then pulled back bullet style, ends form collar

Legs: Round rubber hackle, cream or color to match natural

Foam Hopper
Originator: Ralph Headrick
Hook: TMC 300, Mustad 79580, sizes 6-12
Thread: Monocord size A, yellow or color to match natural
Body: Yellow pre-cut closed cell foam, folded and extend over sides of hook shank, then segmented
Wing: Turkey tail feather sprayed with clear acrylic, cut to shape
Head: Natural deer hair, tied forward then pulled back to form bullet head, butts from head form collar, clip from bottom
Legs: Yellow rubber hackle

Bibliography

Arbona, Jr., Fred L. *Mayflies, the Angler, and the Trout*. Tulsa: Winchester Press, 1980.

Borger, Gary A. *Designing Trout Flies*. Wausau: Tomorrow River Press, 1991.

Chan, Brian M. *Flyfishing Strategies for Stillwaters*. Portland: Frank Amato Publications, Inc., 1991.

Cordes, Ron, and Randall Kaufmann. *Lake Fishing with a Fly*. Portland: Frank Amato Publications, Inc., 1984.

Davy, Alf, ed. *'The Gilly' A Flyfisher's Guide*. Kelowna, B.C. Alf Davy, 1985.

Dennis, Jr., Jack. *Tying Flies with Jack Dennis and Friends*. Jackson: Snake River Books, 1993.

Hafele, Rick, and Dave Hughes. *The Complete Book of Western Hatches*. Portland: Frank Amato Publications, Inc., 1981.

Hafele, Rick, and Scott Roederer. *Aquatic Insects and Their Imitations*. Boulder: Johnson Books, 1987.

Hughes, Dave: *American Fly Tying Manual*. Portland: Frank Amato Publications, Inc., 1986.

Hughes, Dave: *Strategies for Stillwater*. Harrisburg: Stackpole Books, 1991.

LaFontaine, Gary. *Caddisflies, New York*: Winchester Press/Nick Lyons Books, 1981.

Kaufmann, Randall. *Tying Nymphs*. Portland: Western Fisherman's Press, 1994.

McCafferty, W. Patrick. *Aquatic Entomology*. Boston: Science Books International, 1981.

Merritt, R.W. and K.W. Cummins. *An Introduction to the Aquatic Insects of North America*. Dubuque: Kendall / Hunt Publishing Co., 1984 (2nd ed.).

Merwin, John, ed. *Stillwater Trout*. New York: Nick Lyons Books, 1980.

Raymond, Steve. *Kamloops*. Portland: Frank Amato Publications, Inc., 1994. (3rd ed.).

Stetzer, Randle S. *Flies: The Best One Thousand*. Portland: Frank Amato Publications, Inc., 1992.

Swisher, Doug and Carl Richards. *Selective Trout*. New York: Crown Publishers, Inc. 1971.

Index